KU-619-257

Contents

Acknowledgements

To Mike, who didn't run a mile when I first suggested adoption and turned out to be the best daddy ever. To my parents, who have always supported me (even when I forgot to thank them in my wedding speech – sorry again). To the rest of my family, who have embraced our son as if he'd been with us since he was born. To our many friends who've been there throughout – you know who you are.

I want to thank our social worker and the team at our son's local authority for believing in us and making it happen. Also his foster carers: award-winning for very good reasons! I'm only sorry that I can't give your real names here for everyone to see.

We couldn't be more grateful to New Family Social, the charity for gay and lesbian adopters, and its members who have supported us – many of whom have become friends. Without them we might not have made it.

Thank you to Shaila Shah at BAAF for the opportunity to write this book and to Hedi Argent for her helpful comments and advice.

The names of most people mentioned in this book have been changed to maintain anonymity.

About the author

Pablo Fernández was born in Spain in 1971 but has lived in the UK since 1995. He lives in the south-east of England with Mike, his partner for 15 years and husband for four, and their son. They don't have any pets because, despite his partner's and his son's insistence on getting one, Pablo has not given in.

For our son

You're my teddy bear!
And I love you to infinity and beyond.

The Our Story series
This book is part of BAAF's Our Story series, which explores adoption and fostering experiences as told by adoptive parents and foster carers.

Also available in the series:
- *An Adoption Diary* by Maria James
- *Flying Solo* by Julia Wise
- *In Black and White* by Nathalie Seymour
- *Adoption Undone* by Karen Carr
- *A Family Business* by Robert Marsden
- *Together in Time* by Ruth and Ed Royce
- *Take Two* by Laurel Ashton
- *Holding on and Hanging in* by Lorna Miles
- *Dale's Tale* by Helen Jayne
- *Frozen* by Mike Butcher
- *When Daisy met Tommy* by Jules Belle
- *Is it True you have Two Mums?* by Ruby Clay
- *As if I was a Real Boy* by Gordon and Jeannie Mackenzie

The series editor
Hedi Argent is an independent family placement consultant, trainer and freelance writer. She is the author of *Find me a Family* (Souvenir Press, 1984), *Whatever Happened to Adam?* (BAAF, 1998), *Related by Adoption* (BAAF, 2004), *One of the Family* (BAAF, 2005), *Ten Top Tips for Placing Children in Permanent Families* (BAAF, 2006), *Josh and Jaz have Three Mums* (BAAF, 2007), *Ten Top Tips for Placing Siblings* (BAAF, 2008), and *Ten Top Tips for Supporting Kinship Placements* (BAAF, 2009). She is the co-author of *Taking Extra Care* (BAAF, 1997, with Ailee Kerrane) and *Dealing with Disruption* (BAAF, 2006, with Jeffrey Coleman), and the editor of *Keeping the Doors Open* (BAAF, 1988), *See You Soon* (BAAF, 1995), *Staying Connected* (BAAF, 2002), and *Models of Adoption Support* (BAAF, 2003). She has also written six illustrated booklets in the children's series published by BAAF: *What Happens in Court?* (2003, with Mary Lane), *What is Contact?* (2004), *What is a Disability?* (2004), *Life Story Work* (2005, with Shaila Shah), *What is Kinship Care?* (2007) and *Adopting a Brother or Sister* (2010).

Foreword

When my partner and I decided to adopt, I looked for publications about gay adoption in the UK. I searched for an adoption blog, or a book that described the day-to-day of the adoption process so I could read how others had felt when they went through it. I couldn't find anything, so I wrote about ours as it happened: the ups and downs, the bureaucracy, the milestones, the doubts, the happy moments, the frustrations...in the hope that it would help anyone else who is thinking of going through the same process or wants to know how it feels.

What follows are excerpts from the diary entries I kept throughout our entire adoption process, from our first enquiry to the day we met our son.

1

Introduction

September 2007

My name is Pablo. I'm 36. I was born and grew up in Spain but have been living in the UK since 1995. In 1996 I met Mike and we've been together since then. Mike is English, and he's 40. We're both what I guess people would call "professionals", with office-based jobs that pay an average salary. In census terms, Mike is white British and I am white European. We live in a town in the south-east of England.

I can't honestly remember when we started to discuss adoption seriously. About five years ago I guess. We talked about it every now and then. Sometimes Mike was more positive, at other times he wasn't. I was always more or less enthusiastic, although I can't say I was ever 100 per cent sure. We kept going around in circles, all the while thinking it was pointless anyway as no one would actually give us a child. We'd never met or even heard of a gay couple adopting! Whatever information I managed to find suggested that it would be extra difficult for us to adopt as a gay couple and that gay adopters tended to be offered the "leftovers": children that nobody else wanted because they had extreme mental or physical problems. This was really offputting.

We looked into intercountry adoption, but most countries refuse same-sex couples and even single men. In any case, most agencies estimate that the cost of an intercountry adoption starts at about £20,000 and Mike and I are not in a position to even think about spending that kind of money.

We never really considered surrogacy because it's not something that can be arranged in the UK. Besides, again, it's hugely expensive and complicated to go abroad to do it. We also never really felt the need to have a child that was genetically ours.

In 2003 I made enquiries at our local council. They suggested we go to a London agency, as they might have more experience of dealing with gay couples. At the time, the Adoption and Children Act 2002 had not come into effect. This meant that only one of us could make the application, and the other one would be treated as "someone else with whom the child lives in the house". We really felt this was not right, but we might have given it serious consideration had we not known that the forthcoming Act would allow unmarried and same-sex couples to apply jointly, so we decided to wait. As it happened, the Act did not come into effect until December 2005, and by then we were starting to plan our wedding, so everything was put on hold.

We got married in Spain in May 2007 (same-sex marriages – as opposed to civil partnerships – became legal in Spain in 2005). After the wedding we started talking about adoption a bit more seriously again. In the end we reached the conclusion that there was never going to be a time when we were both 100 per cent sure that adoption was the right thing for us. The uncertainties and changing factors are so many that it would be impossible. The difference this time was that instead of just letting the matter drop for another few months as we'd done before, we decided that we would do something about it. Make enquiries, start the application process, even get approved by a panel...all those things don't mean that you have to take a child on if you are not sure. We could always stop the process if we changed our minds.

So why do it? We must be such traditional guys that a few months after getting married we've started going on about having children! I suppose it's quite a natural thing to do. You get to that age in your mid-thirties when all your (heterosexual) friends have children. I always wanted to have children. Then I accepted that I was gay and thought that it was not to be, which to me was one of the hardest things about coming out.

But the more I thought about it, the more I realised that this needn't be the case. I love children. I love playing with my friends' kids and with my nephew and nieces. It feels quite natural to me. It's what people do, isn't it? They have children. I don't see why I shouldn't have a paternal instinct just because I'm gay. I want to look after a child (or children). I want to bring them up, educate them, watch them grow, support them, share their joy in the good times and cry with them in the bad times. I want to be a grandfather one day (but not too soon!). I know Mike and I would make good parents.

Mike struggles with this still. He worries that we'll get the child from hell who will burn the house down on the first day. More importantly, he worries that because we're a gay couple, we'll be imposing something on the children that will make them stand out: they'll get called names at school, get picked on. I tell him that they'll probably get picked on anyway. They could have big ears, or red hair, or whatever else you get picked on at school for. And whilst coming home to two dads may not be the ideal family they are dreaming of as they sit in a foster home waiting to be adopted, surely it has to beat not being adopted at all.

We know there will be intrusions and difficult moments. That it will be hard, and emotional, full of doubts and life-changing, whatever the outcome. We'll find out a lot about ourselves. We'll have to make tough decisions. We also know that we'll have doubts and change our minds back and forth a million times. But that is the process we are starting; and maybe at the end of it there will be more than two of us in our family.

2

2007

Wednesday 3rd October

After much deliberation, Mike finally emailed the Children and Families Unit at the council in a nearby town today. We've been advised not to approach our local council, since agencies don't want to place children in the area where they lived before they were taken into care. This, I guess, is to avoid coming across the birth family in the supermarket whilst doing the shopping. A private agency was out of the question from the start as most are religious agencies. Although current legislation states that they cannot exclude us because of our sexuality, we feel that we don't want the people with whom we will be closely involved to accept us reluctantly. We've been honest and have already stated that we are a gay couple. After all the emotion, stress and doubts, it ended up being quite a straightforward email and a bit of an anticlimax, really. But here is where it officially starts and, though filled with anxiety about how it will all turn out, we are excited about it.

Saturday 27th October

The adoption team have sent us some information leaflets

and a form to indicate in writing if we are interested in attending an initial interview. We've said yes, of course.

Friday 16th November
We've received a letter from the council about the initial interview. 'You will be given an opportunity to hear about adoption as well as being invited to discuss your personal circumstances. Hopefully at this stage we will be able to advise you whether an application to social services is appropriate and you will be given an opportunity to decide whether you wish to take the application to the next stage'. So basically it's like the first audition for *The X Factor*: they get a first impression and if it's no good you're out! The letter says that they are very busy at the moment and it will be a few weeks before they can arrange a date for the interview. This is fine as it gives us a chance to prepare and think things through a bit more. Let's just hope the interviewers are nothing like the *X Factor* judges!

Friday 21st December
Just had a thought that this could be our last Christmas on our own. It's unlikely really, as I'm sure the process will take longer than a year, but I guess it's possible.

3

2008

Friday 18th January

Another letter arrived from social services today. They would like us to go for an initial interview on 30th January. It will be with the team manager of the Adoption team and another colleague. In the last letter they said we'd discuss our personal circumstances. No idea what kind of things they'll ask, so no idea how to prepare for it. I suppose there'll be things like boy or girl, age, background, why we want to do it...and I'm not sure we have answers for any of those questions. We have some more serious talking to do.

Sunday 20th January

Today we discussed whether we should move to a bigger house. We had a similar discussion a few weeks ago about converting the loft. But in the end it boils down to the same point: what exactly do we need another bedroom for? It all depends on whether we end up adopting or not. And if so, how many children? There are so many uncertainties. It's not so much about whether we will go ahead than about which and how many, if any, child or children we'll be matched with. We could get the perfect house with lots of bedrooms and a big car to fit buggies or booster seats and still find that we're not approved, or that if approved, we're not offered a good match or we're offered children with certain disabilities that we're not equipped to care for. Not that we can afford a new house or a new car anyway. Today is one of those days when you realise your life is completely on hold throughout the process. I suppose this is OK, just as long as it doesn't drag on for years.

Wednesday 30th January
We had our initial interview today. Two social workers greeted us and we went into an unwelcoming, hot, tiny interview room with mucky seats with the foam coming out of the cushions. They asked us about our reasons for wanting to adopt. It felt like a job interview. I kept thinking that I should try and think of good answers, but we just gave really honest answers, which I guess is what we were meant to do. At one point Mike was a little too honest and said he didn't want a "grizzling lump" to look after, which I thought was pretty much our interview over and our case closed before opening.

They explained the process: once invited to apply, you complete the application form a few weeks before the preparation course. These are four days in which everything is gone over in detail and adopters come and talk about their experience. After the preparation course comes the home study: between six and eight interviews (one individually, the rest together). They run police checks, contact referees and then you need to pass a medical. After this, they make a recommendation to their adoption panel. If all goes well you are approved and go on a waiting list. If, after three months on the waiting list, no child or children have been linked with you, then your paperwork is released to neighbouring councils and to the Adoption Register for England and Wales. If there is a match, then the planning stage starts, when you see pictures or videos of the children, make visits and talk to the foster carers, until the child or children move in. They told us that single men and gay and lesbian couples tend to wait one or two years.

After all this, they left the room to discuss our application and came back a few minutes later to tell us that they would accept it. Relief! We have been told to think about references and about our support network. We should also get more experience of being with children, like volunteering in playgroups.

We came out of the meeting absolutely mentally exhausted but really happy to have got through. There was so much to take in. The other thing they said was that they had recently placed a child with another gay couple, so we're not the first ones to go through the process with them, which is reassuring. I think at some point I may ask if we can get in touch with them. It would be nice to meet other gay adopters.

Thursday 31st January

We spent yesterday thinking about who our referees could be and weighing up who would be good because they have known us the longest, or because they have children themselves. We also discussed who would be the primary carer. We've agreed it would be me, partly because of my work, which is more flexible and requires less travel than Mike's, partly because it feels right for us. Today I talked to my line manager (who is also a friend) about our adoption plans. She was supportive and pleased for us, although a little surprised. I asked her about taking adoption leave and she sent me all the information.

She's one of the first people I've told. We have kept this mostly to ourselves as we wanted to be really sure before we told anyone. It's a bit like people not telling other people that they are pregnant until after the three-month scan. You don't want to get anyone's hopes up in case of disappointment and you need to get used to the idea yourself.

Tuesday 19th February

Mike has received an email from the adoption team saying that the next preparation course may be full, in which case we'd have to wait until October. I rang them and they are going to see if we can get on an earlier one. Having to wait eight months for the preparation course would mean that we could do volunteering work at a school or nursery and be more confident by the time we get to the preparation course stage, but it also feels like ages away. We've wasted so much time dithering that we just want to get on with it now.

Sunday 24th February

For the last few days we've been talking about how we keep having second and third and fourth thoughts about the adoption. I'm not worried about this, though. I think it's healthy to have doubts and a lot of it is that we don't want to be disappointed.

We filled in the "expression of interest form" today. We wondered whether it mattered who was applicant number one and who was number two (I was number one in the end). We discussed how many siblings we would want to be matched with (we wrote "two" following the golden rule of "never have more children than hands") and their ages. Mike was a bit reluctant to say 'from zero'; he's not keen on the idea of a baby (I think he wants a child who can tell you why they're crying), whereas I am, although I probably find it as scary as he does! Not that we would ever be matched with a young baby anyway, so this is a bit academic. Mike suggested a maximum age of eight, which I was surprised about as I thought four or five would be the oldest he'd go for. Somehow eight seems a little too old to overcome whatever circumstance has put the child in care, but we went with that so as not to close any doors at this stage.

Friday 29th February

I'm in Spain at the moment visiting my family. We haven't told either of our families yet. It somehow makes it so definite to tell them. I don't want to get their hopes up (assuming they receive the news as good news) and I also wonder whether we should keep this private for a while longer. If I tell them it would mean that every time they ring they'll ask if there is any news. And there probably won't be. Or they won't ask and I'll get annoyed that they're not asking...

Saturday 1st March

I spoke to Mike on the phone this evening. We have been given a place on the preparation course in April! It's good news, yet I'm not looking forward to it. I know it will be totally emotionally draining and we'll come out possibly more confused than when we went in. There's also the issue of how other prospective adopters will react to us. I like to think that everyone is fine with gay people nowadays, but they may not quite react the same to the idea of gay men adopting. I wonder if they'll think we are somehow less deserving.

Sunday 2nd March

I made my mind up today to tell my family about our plans to adopt. Having the dates for the preparation course makes it more real and there's more to share with them. After lunch I told everyone about our plans. It felt like coming out all over again. They really weren't expecting it. They had some questions about the legal process and where we'd be adopting from (in Spain most people adopt from abroad).

Later in the afternoon Mum and I sat in the kitchen and she told me she thought the adoption was a good idea and that she was sure we had thought long and hard about it. I told her that we are not getting our hopes up, how we don't want to compromise too much in terms of physical or mental disability, and how age could be an issue as language is very important to me and I really want children to be able to communicate with the family, and their cousins in particular. If they are "too old", learning Spanish might have to wait and never be fully achieved.

I am glad I told them, although I know it will worry them somewhat. But they have been supportive and received the news well, so that's one less thing for me to worry (too much) about.

Friday 7th March

I'm back in the UK. Today I had a look at the papers that the adoption team sent while I was away. They are the authorisation for criminal records checks and we need to list our referees. I'm still not looking forward to the daunting prospect of the April preparation course. I'm convinced that they'll do their best to put people off during the course. Not because they don't want adopters, but because they'll want to make sure that we know what we're getting into. At the initial interview one of the social workers told us a terrible story of a little girl who they believe was sexually abused and I keep thinking about her. It made me feel really sad and I wonder how we'd cope with a child from such a background.

Sunday 9th March

We went for lunch with my oldest UK friends yesterday. We told them about the adoption (and asked them to be referees), and they were very encouraging. Much like coming out, it's getting easier the more people we tell. It's quite hard in a way, though, because you tell people and they say very nice things about you, how brave you are, what great parents they think you'll make...which is very nice to hear. But we then have to add the caveats: 'It may never actually happen as a lot can go wrong along the way, we may not be approved, we may not be matched, it may take many years'...which sort of spoils the mood. It's like 'Here's our news but it may not be news at all', and it's kind of weird.

Thursday 13th March
We filled in the "proper" application forms yesterday and today Mike took the forms to the local authority with passports and bills to prove our identity. We decided that Mike's mother and my brother would be the family referees and the others would be close friends who have children.

Friday 4th April
We both feel we can picture some aspects of having a child or children in the house and being part of our lives, but not the day-to-day business of going to nursery or school, picking them up and that sort of thing. I think at the moment we are so focused on the actual process of adopting that trying to imagine children being here is hard: do we try to picture ourselves with a baby, a toddler, a young child, or an older child? A boy or a girl? One or two?

Anyway, *Children who Wait* arrived today. It's the publication from Adoption UK – an organisation run by and for adopters – that lists children's profiles. We subscribed to it a while ago even though it's very early days. Mike and I looked at it together. It provokes such mixed feelings in me. It's like a catalogue of children. You find yourself drawn to some and dismissing others because of some stupid reason – like you might pick shirts by mail order. It's awful. Some of the children I would take home with me right now if I could. Others I feel sorry for; they look like it's just too late for them. Reading some of the profiles between the lines makes me wonder if we'll ever be able to deal with some of the issues these children have. We'll revisit all this during the home study, I guess.

There was an article in *Adoption Today* about a lesbian

in France who was barred from adopting a child. The decision by the French court has been overturned as it was discriminatory. This could have an effect on EU laws. At the moment only nine EU countries allow gay and lesbian couples to adopt: the UK, Spain, Germany, Belgium, Iceland, Norway, Sweden and the Netherlands. We think we have it hard, but at least we're in countries where we are allowed to apply in the first place!

Monday 7th April

The first day of the preparation course is tomorrow and we're getting nervous. What will it be like? I'm not so concerned about the content of the course, although I hope it's not too offputting or hard-hitting. I don't want to get too emotional but I don't want to appear distant either. I'm more worried about everyone else on the course. What if they have a problem with us being there? I hope we don't have to do too much "workshop-type" stuff where everyone has to share and all that. But at the same time it would be great to meet other couples who are going through the same thing and being able to talk about it.

Not feeling very positive today and I almost asked Mike if he wants to forget about it all, but was worried that he'd say yes.

Tuesday 8th April

Mike decided to go the "back route" to the preparation course and we arrived five minutes late. I wasn't feeling as negative as I did last night, but I was still nervous about meeting the other prospective adopters. There were ten of us: four heterosexual couples and Mike and me. If anyone objected to us, they didn't say a word. I didn't even catch a raised eyebrow. We all sat in a row and were introduced to the three social workers who were leading the course, including Miranda, the Senior Practitioner, and one of the social workers we met at our initial interview.

The social workers introduced themselves, welcomed us and handed out a pack with the schedule for the four days. We worked in groups and everyone seems really nice. After all the concerns I had about everyone else, they turned out to be quite normal, as you would expect. I felt silly that I'd worried about whether they'd be homophobic or react badly to us.

The second session in the afternoon was about parenting roles and what they are looking for in adopters. There was a section on children in care, how they got to be in care, and the backgrounds they usually come from.

Conversation during lunch and the breaks was a bit stilted, but it seems that most of the couples are also at the stage where they are still thinking about it and want to find out more, rather than 100 per cent sure that they want to go ahead. This was very reassuring.

We broke up just before four. We didn't speak much on the way home. We were both processing everything we'd heard. I was hoping that Mike would feel more positive today. I am definitely more sure than yesterday. Mike said he had no problem with the process, but still felt unsure about whether we can actually do it. I can't help thinking that he's gone off the idea and he's preparing me for the worst. He can be difficult to read sometimes. I really want to do this, but it has to be because the two of us want to do it.

Wednesday 9th April
I spoke to Mike last night and he said he is just not 100 per cent sure about whether to adopt or not and he hopes he will be able to make his mind up by the end of the preparation course, but he will not go through with this just to humour me. I pushed a bit more later on, and it turns out that his biggest concern is not about wanting to adopt, but about being a good dad. I honestly don't know how to get this through to him: I am sure he would make an excellent dad. Anyone who has seen him interacting with

his best friend's children could tell you that. He would make a better dad than me. Maybe better is not the right word. I'm pretty sure I'd end up being the disciplinarian and the one doing the educational activities and Mike would be the one messing about. I think both roles are necessary and can complement one another, but he'll be the favourite. Anyway, I am much more at ease now, as I was really worried that he might want to pull out. I think his fears about his ability to be a good dad are valid, but in a completely different league to not wanting to adopt. I've told him that whatever decision he takes must be his own, and not to please me in any way.

Today the course seemed to go better than yesterday. The group was more comfortable and interacted better. In the morning we discussed attachment, displacement and bonding. In the afternoon it was all about education, qualities of good parents, managing behaviour and positive parenting. We were really exhausted by the end of it, but feeling quite positive. It's just as well the last two days of the course are not for another two weeks.

Sunday 13th April
Spoke to my mum and dad today. They were asking about the preparation course and the process. They are concerned for us, worried that taking on a child or children with the type of baggage they tend to come with might be too much of a strain on our relationship. I tried to reassure them, but of course it's hard to reassure someone when you're worried yourself about how you'll cope with a child who might not accept your love, or whose needs are so great that you may not be able to provide for them.

Sunday 20th April
We went to our friends, Gavin and Sue, for dinner on Saturday. They are also adopting, but they're much further ahead than we are. We had a lovely evening and we talked

lots about adoption. It was so nice to hear that they went through more or less every thought process that we've been through (except obviously those that are gay-related): how many children, age, sex, backgrounds…We swapped anecdotes and stories from our experiences so far and they gave us some information and books to read. They are with a Catholic agency, and apparently their promotional literature says something like 'We welcome applications from everyone but if you're gay we'll pass you on to someone else'. They are going to the panel in June, and their social worker has implied they will be approved, and has told them that they could start looking! Sue has been to a family-finding event already. It's such an amazing time for them and they look so happy and excited.

We're actually looking forward to the last two days of the preparation course. It will be nice to see everyone in the group again. It's supposed to be a hard day, as we are doing attachment and abuse, so I guess we will be exposed to some realities that we may not want to think about. We'll see. I am taking a brand-new packet of tissues with me just in case.

Monday 21st April
Third day of the preparation course. The first session wasn't as hard as we thought it might be, although it did deal with abuse and attachment. We then looked at identity issues and life story books. Some of the life stories were quite hard to read, but I think we all managed to keep going without shedding tears. It was sort of weird, because some of us resorted to humour as a way of dealing with what we were reading and discussing. Looking back it feels inappropriate, but I guess it was our coping mechanism.

Also I accessed the Adoption UK messageboard for the first time today. It's silly really as we have subscribed to the magazine for ages, but I never thought to log on until someone mentioned it at the course today. There is a gay and lesbian adoption section which looks like it will be really helpful.

Tuesday 22nd April

Final day of the preparation course today. In the morning we discussed contact with the birth family. We read a very moving letter from a birth father who is in prison, and other stuff that made us realise how important contact is, even if the idea of being in touch with the birth family is a bit weird. We also went through the introductions process, when you meet the children, start going to their foster home and then they visit you until they are finally placed with you. The last bit before lunch was a talk about after-adoption support. The afternoon was quite emotional and the best bit by far. A mother, father and adopted daughter came to tell us about their family and the story of how they came together. They showed us their family photos and told us about issues they'd had and continue to have. Another adoptive mum told us her story, which had gone without a hiccup, and then a father of a little girl told us his family's story. It was all very touching; we were shown photos and those children looked beautiful, just like any other happy children playing in the park, or with their brothers and sisters. This was the best thing ever. After all the doom and gloom of the warnings of what can go wrong, it was great to hear and see these happy families. We said our goodbyes and drove home feeling really optimistic and full of energy rather than drained, as we had left on the previous days.

My only complaint would be how geared up towards heterosexual families the preparation course is. One of the presenters did make an allusion to "having two daddies" as a nod to us, but even a questionnaire we had to fill in at the end asked us about whether we'd been through IVF, which clearly would not apply to a male gay couple.

Now that the preparation course is over, we have to

confirm whether we want to go ahead or not. They've told us that the best thing we can do is to volunteer in an organisation where we can get more experience of looking after children. Mike has contacted a local school about being a volunteer reader and also the Boy Scouts, and I am going to ask at one of the nurseries near my work.

Monday 28th April
My brother and sister-in-law came over to England on Tuesday night with my nephew, who is seven, and my niece, who is five. They went sightseeing on Wednesday and Thursday while we were at work and then on Friday we went to Legoland and had a great time going on all the attractions. At the weekend we did lots of stuff together. It has been such a lovely visit, especially considering my brother and I were never close when we were teenagers. I think it was good for Mike to spend time with the kids as well. They really got on with him and managed to communicate with their few words of English and Mike doing his best with his Spanish.

Tuesday 29th April
Last night I read a thread on the Adoption UK messageboards where one member asked whether anyone had regrets about adopting. Most people didn't, although many said that it had been difficult. One person gave a cryptic "yes" and another said they would have made different choices. This left me rather deflated, as I'd been on a high since the last day of the preparation course. Do birth parents ever regret having children? Do they reconsider their decision to have children while still trying to conceive? I guess some fathers may wonder whether they'll make good fathers throughout the pregnancy. I suppose for mothers it tends to be more natural, although I am sure it happens too. What about couples who have an unplanned pregnancy? Do they have regrets afterwards?

Anyway, back to the messageboard: more people had contributed and it was a bit upsetting to read about failed placements and negative experiences, but we need to be very aware of this side of the coin as well.

I finally had an interview with a local preschool nursery today. They were really nice and seemed keen. I'll be going one afternoon a week to help out with activities. It's quite exciting and just a little bit terrifying as well.

Thursday 8th May
I spoke on the phone today to another gay guy who's in the process with the same local authority as we are. He and his partner have had lots of confrontations with their social worker. They were told they'd only be considered to adopt children who are eight or nine, despite the fact that they've expressed a preference for nought to three. He really got the feeling that they are trying to put them off. Apparently their social worker kept referring to "normal" couples when talking about heterosexual couples and also told them that when children are available they 'look more favourably upon heterosexual couples'. Don't know what to make of all this. Our experience has not been like that at all. How much is it their social worker? How much the fact they are gay? Or is it something to do with the personal circumstances of this couple in particular?

Friday 9th May
Mike is volunteering with a local Beaver group. He went for his first day yesterday and he really enjoyed himself. I'm looking forward to my first day at the school, but am also a bit nervous in case I mess anything up. How will the children take to me?

Saturday 10th May
Children who Wait arrived again today. I read through it and once more had incredibly mixed feelings about this

"catalogue" of children. Some were born in 1994 which means they are 14 years old. The thought of those children still being in care at that age is just so sad. It may be that they've been in the care system for years or maybe they went into care at quite an "old" age, but I just can't imagine that adoptive parents would want to take on a teenager. Every time I see this magazine, I end up reconsidering every idea I have about what sort of children we would be able to adopt. I was about to write 'we would accept' and that seems so wrong. I'm clearly not *au fait* with the terminology. It's like during the first day of the preparation course, when one of the prospective adopters referred to "ordering" a baby. She immediately corrected herself, we all laughed and it really broke the ice, but I understand how easy it is to think in those terms.

Anyhow, there was this lovely eight-year-old girl who reminded me of one of my nieces. I don't know if it was the physical resemblance, but I was instantly drawn to her. I've always imagined five or six as our maximum age, and I tend to think that we'd have boys and not girls, but there I was, picturing her with us, even though she doesn't at all fit with our ideas. At least it means that we are quite open-minded.

Monday 12th May
Today was my first day at nursery school. I was met by the teacher I will be supporting and she introduced me to the kids. There were eleven of them, all four years old. I played Lego with four or five of them first and then went outside to do "magic paint", which involves painting a wall with water. It's never-ending and the kids don't seem to get tired of it! Then we played in the shade for a bit, drawing, colouring and cutting out paper, played with toy cars and tidied up. I read the kids a story (after the teacher asked me if I could read in English – I tried hard not to take offence) and then they sang a couple of songs for us. The two-and-a-half hours went by very quickly. It was a really nice

afternoon and I felt very welcome. I was a bit nervous that I wouldn't cope, or that they'd hate me instantly, but that was so not the case. Although I did hear quite a few variations of my name! I'm already looking forward to next Monday.

Wednesday 14th May
Through the Adoption UK messageboards I heard of New Family Social, a gay adopters' organisation that arranges meet-ups and has its own online advice forum. I applied for membership and it was confirmed today. We've never been the sort of people who only want to hang out with other gay people or go to gay-only venues, and the vast majority of our friends are heterosexual, but I guess because there aren't that many gay adopters it's good to meet others in a similar situation. When we started this, we felt like "the only prospective gay adopters in the village" and it's a comfort to know there are more of us and, most importantly, others who've successfully adopted already.

Thursday 15th May
We went to the pub this evening with Sue, our friend and fellow prospective adopter, and two of the couples we met at the preparation course. The adoption team weren't too keen on us keeping in touch, because we could end up being considered for the same children, but we had swapped phone numbers anyway. It was very nice to see these couples again. It turns out we all had the same first impression of Miranda, the social worker who led the course, and we all said we wouldn't be too keen to be allocated to her, as she came across as quite bossy and cold.

Sue told us that their social worker has been off sick, so their panel has been put back for a couple of months. It must be so frustrating and disappointing for them. Also, Mike and I had understood that the adoption team would be writing to us to ask whether we wanted to go ahead or not, but it turns out that we don't need to wait for them to write and we can just let them know. One of the couples confirmed straight away and they have already been allocated a social worker. The other couple have replied too, although they haven't heard back yet.

Saturday 17th May

Today we talked more about whether to go ahead now or wait a bit longer. At the end of the preparation course we had decided to delay before giving a definite "yes" as we knew they wanted us to have more experience with children. But considering how long it takes them to get going, we're wondering whether it may not be best to say "yes" now and keep volunteering while we wait. At the end of the day, the home study will last months, so we might as well start it sooner rather than later. We keep going around in circles, though. It feels very definite to say "yes" at this point, when we still find it so hard to picture what our lives will be like if we adopt. Are we well enough equipped or prepared to take it all on? Are we ready? I suppose that's for the social worker and the panel to decide. I personally think that we've done all the thinking and talking we can do and what we need to do now is just go for it, but that's not the way Mike deals with things. He always wants to be absolutely sure before he embarks on something, even more so for something as important as this. The funny thing is that I don't think he is any less keen than I am, he is just more cautious. So I need to let him have his time to keep pondering, but not forever. We've reached a compromise and decided to make the decision in early June, when I get back from Spain (I'll be off there to do some work in a few days).

Saturday 24th May

The Criminal Records Bureau (CRB) checks from our

local authority arrived yesterday. At last! They were all clear. At least I know Mike hasn't been hiding any skeletons in his closet!

I saw an ad today for a really interesting post. The job description fits well with my CV and I fancy the sort of role that it would involve. But it would mean commuting every day and not working from home (as I can do now), which is not ideal if we're going to adopt. After thinking about it all day I've decided not to apply. This is yet another of those things that has to be put on hold until we know whether we'll ever be approved or matched with a child. It's not the end of the world, but it's frustrating how much is affected by a decision that ultimately is not up to us.

Monday 26th May

Yesterday we booked a big holiday for next March. It's actually our honeymoon, as we never really had a chance to go on a proper holiday last year. Today I woke up thinking that if we had children we could not plan to go on holiday just like that, or have friends round and improvise dinner as we did at the weekend. For the first time in ages I had a moment of wondering why the hell we want to do this and why we can't just be content with the way things are. After Mike woke up I talked to him about it and he reassured me. It's nice that we don't have low moments at the same time! I hope we're not the only ones who have moments like these. Surely not everyone is 100 per cent sure all of the time? Or maybe they are and I should worry...

Sunday 1st June

I'm working in Spain at the moment and staying with my family. Today we went out to a restaurant with my parents, my brother, my sister-in-law and their kids. After lunch we went over to the playground in the park opposite and I played with the kids while their parents had a break. We had a really good time on all the slides and I was quite relieved at being able to keep up with a four, a five, and a seven-year-old at the same time!

When we got back the eldest played up and spent most of the afternoon and evening being difficult: refusing to do as he was asked, not listening, and hitting the others, and by the time they went we were all exhausted! My sister-in-law shot me a look as if to say 'And you want kids?'

Monday 2nd June
After lunch I picked up the kids from school and spent the afternoon with them. This was my first time on my own with the three of them. We actually had a really good time playing with the Wii, doing puzzles, drawing, and playing hide-and-seek, but it was hard work to keep an eye on them and somehow keep them entertained. I was running out of ideas by the end and that was only for three hours!

Wednesday 4th June
Last day of my visit to Spain. My brother, sister-in-law, and the kids came over for dinner. The middle one was playing up this time and just wouldn't eat her dinner. The eldest was also being a bit difficult and kept hitting everyone. I thought to myself that if they were adopted, I would be wondering what had happened in their past to make them behave this way, or what the books say about that kind of behaviour, or maybe whether I should be ringing the social worker. But as it happens I know these kids, I know they haven't had any trauma in their lives, and at the end of the day, kids have good days and bad days and they behave one way or another for no particular reason. I'll need to remember this when we have our own children!

Thursday 5th June
I flew back to the UK today. I opened the post and there was a letter from our local authority asking us to get back to them by the 16th with our decision about whether we

want to go ahead with the home study or not. In a way it's nice to have a deadline, otherwise we'd keep considering pros and cons forever! Our options are to say "yes", "no", or to say we'd like to get back to them after the summer. We're going to a New Family Social meet-up on Sunday and we've decided to wait until then before we make up our minds.

Sunday 8th June

We went to London for the New Family Social group meeting. We were feeling a bit nervous about it, especially as we've been having so many doubts lately. We got there, signed up and then chatted to a Spanish guy I've been in touch with through Adoption UK and his partner. They have a lovely five-year-old boy. Then we chatted to another couple who'll be going to the panel soon, a couple who've just adopted two boys, as well as other people at different stages in the process. It was great meeting everyone and seeing how many gay people are around who have adopted successfully or are hoping to do so. It was truly inspiring to meet them and most of all to see how "normal" their kids were. After the preparation course and reading all the books about the children who are in care, we had this image of "damaged" children who nobody would be able to control. What we saw today was fantastic kids playing in the park, being kids, and as "normal" as they get. To actually see gay and lesbian parents just being families, playing, telling kids not to eat the sweets, to stay within sight, to play nicely, and chasing after them when they pay no attention – just like any other kid – was amazing. Suddenly adoption just seemed a very real thing with real people, and not a million unanswerable questions.

When we got home we wrote a letter to our local authority to confirm that yes, we will be going ahead with the home study. I'm so glad that we've made a decision at last and happy that I am feeling enthusiastic again. Mike feels the same way. The best thing about it is that for the first time we can imagine ourselves being a family. We can actually see it happening and that makes today the best day since we started this process.

Monday 30th June
It's been three weeks now since we wrote back to our local authority to confirm we wanted to go ahead and we haven't heard from them at all. Now that we've made the decision we're keen to move on and maybe start on the home study before I go away for the summer. I have to work in Spain for several weeks and will only be in the UK for a few days here and there, so unless something happens soon, we probably won't get started until September, which would be a pity.

Wednesday 2nd July
Yesterday we decided that we'd given our local authority enough time already and rang them. We've been allocated a social worker. It's Miranda, who led the preparation course. At first we weren't too sure how we felt about her. During the preparation course she was very cold, business-like and matter-of-fact, whereas the other social workers were much friendlier. At one point she even told a couple of us off for taking too long to come back from our coffee break! However, she is a senior practitioner and we're very confident that there won't be any mistakes or oversights if we have her, as she is very experienced and has put many couples through panel (no gay couples though). So we feel it may be a bit hard to open up to her, but we think we will be in good hands. We have to ring her tomorrow to try and organise the first home visit, so hopefully we'll get the whole thing underway before I go to Spain.

Thursday 3rd July
I spoke to Miranda today. She's coming to see us for the

first interview on Wednesday. We're both excited but also a bit nervous. We're convinced she'll come in with white gloves on and check for dust specks on top of the wardrobes, rust inside the washing machine drum or something like that. I know they say they're not expecting you to, but something tells me there'll be some major cleaning going on on Tuesday evening...

Wednesday 9th July

Well, that's another milestone that we can tick off the list! We spent some time on Tuesday night going over Form F (now called the Prospective Adopter's Report) to try and work out what sorts of questions we might get from our social worker.

As soon as she arrived (five minutes early – trying to catch us out?) Miranda asked to see the house and the garden. She didn't pull out any white gloves or check for dust mites, and she seemed to like it. Then we sat down and we talked about what voluntary work we've been doing and what adoption books we've read.

To be fair to Miranda, she was not at all like we were dreading. She was funny, reassuring, smiley, and warm. I guess she is the sort of person who works better on a one-to-one basis. Because of my nerves I just kept talking and talking. It was like verbal diarrhoea. I could hear myself doing it and Mike kept shooting me looks but I just could not shut up. It was quite awful. But not as awful as when I asked her if she had a problem with gay men adopting. I had meant to ask in a roundabout way whether she thought our being gay might be an issue for her department, but instead what came out was a rather more direct question aimed at her. I could feel Mike murdering me with a look. Miranda didn't seem to be too fazed and replied that she didn't. She has dealt with placing a child with a gay couple before, and it's been more a case of not many gay couples applying to our local authority rather than anything else.

At some point I must have stopped to draw breath long enough for Mike to make the most of it and end the conversation. We thanked her for coming and saw her out. We are both very relieved and happy with the way it went (well, except for when I didn't stop talking and was almost rude with my directness) and looking forward to working with Miranda.

Mike will have his individual interview in a couple of weeks, but mine won't be until late September due to our conflicting schedules. Miranda will be on holiday when I am back in the country, so it'll have to wait.

Sunday 20th July

I'm back in Spain doing some work and staying with my parents. Now that we're sure we're going ahead and we're into the home study, I'm telling more people and their reactions are great, even if some express concern about our coping with difficult children. The more I talk about it, the more I begin to comprehend what these children have lived through.

Mike has had to stay in the UK working, and he's preparing his family tree and personal story for his individual interview. He's into family history and has researched a lot about his ancestors, so Miranda may get information overload from him rather than me this time!

Monday 21st July

Today I went to see my brother and his family. Also visiting were my eldest niece's best friend, her parents and adopted brother. He is four and came from Russia when he was eleven months old with quite severe developmental delay and ill health. He's still suffering some delay, which is not obvious at all. He's come a long way and is a lovely little boy who interacts really well with the other kids and with adults. He showed me his toy cars; just like my nephew at his age, he seems to be obsessed with red cars and fire engines! I wanted to have a chance to talk to his parents about their adoption and any advice they might have, but the opportunity never really arose.

Friday 25th July

Yesterday I got to speak with the couple who adopted the little Russian boy. We talked for over an hour. They have absolutely no regrets and are delighted with their little boy. The advice they stressed most was "have patience". One thing that was reassuring was to hear that they'd had doubts about whether they were doing the right thing and making the right choices. It seems that this is very normal. Apparently they met regularly with the other people in their preparation course and it was a common thing with all of them.

The day was rounded off nicely with an email from two of the guys we met at the New Family Social get-together last month and with whom we have kept in touch. They have been approved by the panel. I'm really pleased for them. It's so good to hear of other couples who successfully achieve what we're heading towards. It's inspiring and encouraging for us.

Monday 4th August

Mike had his individual interview with Miranda last week. It all went quite well while they were talking about his childhood and family tree, and Miranda was fine with the fact that Mike's relationship with his brother is distant, but when it came to his relationship with his father it was different. Mike's father knows he is gay and they have an amicable relationship, but his father has never asked about me or expressed an interest in meeting me. He didn't come to our wedding either. Miranda said that the panel would not like that at all, as grandparents are very important. She's worried about what we might say to children about why Mike's dad isn't part of their lives. I think many children who are waiting to be adopted come from backgrounds where fathers may be absent from their lives (or even not known), so in fact it could be something they can relate to. And for all we know, Mike's father may come around once he hears he's got another grandson or granddaughter, who knows?

Mike is quite upset and concerned that his father's failure to acknowledge me may be an obstacle to our being approved. His mother, in contrast, is really excited about it and very supportive, as are both my parents.

Monday 11th August
Back in the UK for a couple of days before I return to Spain. One thing that we keep coming back to, especially as it's a question that many people ask when we tell them about our plans to adopt, is whether we want boys or girls. During her first visit, Miranda mentioned that there are normally more boys than girls waiting to be adopted and that placing a girl with a male gay couple was tricky. We don't have a preference as such, but the more we talk about it, the more we feel we might be better prepared for boys. I think it's just that we've been there before ourselves, so we know what growing up being a boy is like. Girls always seem so complicated...and of course neither of us has any idea how to dress a girl, or comb her hair, let alone explain anything when she hits puberty. We have lots of female friends and some have offered to help out, explain things, go shopping for clothes or teach us how to do their hair, but somehow it feels like it would be harder to relate to girls. Having said that, neither of us is into football either, so I think we're stereotyping a bit and making assumptions.

The other thing, of course, is that this is not so much about what *we* want or would like, but about what's best for the kids. And here's where we hit a bit of a bump because we feel that a girl might cope better with having two dads. I think other kids would be less likely to bully a girl for having two dads than they would a boy. A boy might be told something along the lines of 'Your dads are gay so you must be gay', which might not happen if we had a girl. Or would it? Do I have a somewhat naïve idea that girls are less vicious than boys?

I think certain people could also assume that we'd bring up a boy to be gay. Chances are that a boy or girl who grows up with gay dads would probably be quite open-minded (I would hope!) about other people's sexuality, but I don't believe that it would affect their own sexuality any more than our own sexual orientation was affected by being brought up by heterosexual parents.

There is something else that worries me a little as well. Unfortunately some people in this world associate gay men with paedophilia. But I presume that the type of person who thinks that way is not going to be bothered whether it's a boy or a girl, they're going to be against gay men adopting, full stop.

I don't think there should be a general rule about whether gay men are better suited to bringing up boys or girls. At the end of the day it should be a case of the right parents for the right children. If a social worker comes to us with boys we'll consider them, if it's girls we'll consider them as well. If it's a boy and a girl, then why not? At the end of the day, most couples don't get to choose when they get pregnant! We'll go with the best match, boy or girl, but this is something that we'll have to keep discussing with our social worker.

Tuesday 12th August
I rang Human Resources at my work today to ask about adoption leave. I was told that I could take two weeks, the same as paternity leave, and my partner could take the full adoption leave (the assumption being that my partner was female). When I explained that there were two men involved and that I would be the main carer, they told me

that only women can take full adoption leave and that a man has never asked for adoption leave where I work (a very large company). I breathed in, counted to ten and asked if she could double check that and get back to me. About an hour later I received an email informing me that one parent (regardless of gender) can take the full adoption leave, which entitles me to 52 weeks (extendable to 56 under certain circumstances): 18 weeks on almost full pay and statutory pay for the next 21 weeks, no pay for the final 13 weeks. I was relieved, but also quite angry at the initial assumption, so I flagged it up with our equality office.

Friday 5th September
Mike came over to Spain mid-August and we went sightseeing for a few days. All around us were families with kids. We kept thinking that maybe in some months that could be us.

The other day I wrote my life story for Miranda, which I need to send to her in preparation for my individual interview. She's given us a three-page list of questions about our childhood to help us write it. The questions are about our family, how we coped when we were upset, whether we suffered any abuse, how we got on at school… The only "problem" is that I had a very happy childhood. I keep wondering if that may make Miranda or the panel think that I won't be able to cope with children who have suffered some sort of trauma in their lives. Is it a hindrance in the adoption process to have had a happy childhood?

Friday 12th September
Back in the UK at last and back to "regular" office-based work. No more travelling until next summer (which hopefully will be my last having to do summer work – parents of young children can be exempted from having to work abroad).

A couple of days ago we got together for pizza with Gavin and Sue, our friends who are also adopting, and Rebecca and Alan, one of the couples we met at the preparation course. Gavin and Sue were approved in August and Rebecca and Alan are due to go to the panel in early November. It was really nice to share stories of the home study and catch up with everyone. We have lots of friends and family who are very supportive, but people who haven't adopted can't quite understand what it's like. Because of this I figured that there would be times when we might feel like we were on our own, but this hasn't been the case at all. On general adoption issues we have Gavin and Sue and the people from the preparation course. And for gay adoptions we have the online communities in Adoption UK and New Family Social, as well as the people we have met face to face at their get-togethers.

Friday 19th September

Both Mike and I returned to our voluntary work in the last few days. Mike is back with Beavers, helping out in their activities one evening a week. He really enjoys it, even when things don't quite go to plan. This week they were supposed to build tents out of newspapers. Well, one of the volunteers brought copies of *The Sun* to use, and of course the kids were all giggling about the "boobies" on page 3. Oops!

I went back to the nursery where I volunteered last term. I will be mostly working with the four and five-year-olds, although I have asked if I can go into the threes and twos as well. Maybe even into the day nursery, where they have babies as young as two months old. It will all be more experience. Anyhow, I was with the fives this week, most of whom I already knew from last term. It was great to see them again, and they all welcomed me as if I'd only been away for a week and not for most of the summer. Last year's fives are now in "proper" school and I missed them; you get so used to them and then they move on. That's why

I don't think I could ever be a foster carer. I get too attached!

Tuesday 23rd September
The other day Mike and I did a little experiment with the *Children who Wait* magazine. We both took the last four issues and looked at them separately; making notes of the children we would consider and not consider adopting. Then we looked at the magazines together and compared notes. It was a relief to see that we're both thinking along the same lines, although we still differ slightly when it comes to ages. We'll probably compromise for somewhere in between. It was really interesting to discuss our perceptions and attitudes towards some of the children and I think it was a very useful exercise.

Wednesday 24th September
My individual interview with Miranda was today. She was really nice and asked me questions about my family tree, childhood, and people who were an influence on me as I was growing up. She also asked about previous relationships and religion. It all went well and I managed not to talk and talk like last time. The only issue she kept coming back to was Mike's relationship with his brother and, more significantly, with his father. She says that she doesn't want children who come from a dysfunctional family to have another dysfunctional family. I was quite insulted by this but didn't let it show. I explained that given that I have never met either Mike's dad or brother (because they don't want to meet me, not the other way around), I don't really consider them to be part of our family. But if they wanted to meet any children we may ever have, they would always be welcome. Miranda says she'll need to discuss this further with the two of us. Overall I'm happy that at least there appear to be no problems with my family background.

One other thing we discussed was the thoughts I had the other day about whether having had a happy childhood was a bad thing. She said not at all, and that whilst it's true that if you have had negative childhood experiences you can use them to relate to the adopted child, having a happy childhood means you have a good model on which to base bringing up children.

Tuesday 30th September

Today we had our second joint interview. The first 90 minutes or so were about our support networks and our relationship. Miranda asked us about people we would contact in case of emergency, or for advice, or services that we may want to contact, and we gave her names and discussed different support groups. She has asked us to draw an "ecomap" of our support network, which will go into the report for the panel. The second half of this session was about our relationship. First were facts like when we met, when we moved in together and when we got married. Then we moved on to more intimate stuff such as what attracted us to one another, what we got out of the relationship, and what we disagree about, as well as a bit about parenting styles.

Up to that point everything was going well. Despite the fact that Miranda can be quite cold and detached, we were very relaxed and comfortable with the questions, even though some were very personal. Then we got to the big issue regarding Mike's father.

Miranda told us that she'd spoken to her supervisor, who is also the panel advisor, and she said that with things as they are we would not get through the panel. We were obviously devastated to hear this. It seems Miranda feels that Mike is somewhat embarrassed by his sexuality because he won't talk to his father about it. She spoke to a gay panel Chair she knows and he also felt that this was a problem. The other problem she foresees is the effect that

Mike's father's rejection of us could have on Mike and me as a couple, me in general, and any children we may adopt.

We replied that regarding the first issue, Mike is completely out to his friends, co-workers, and relatives such as aunts, uncles and cousins, and his father is the only one he hasn't told in person. Mike has been out to his mother for years, and it was she who told his dad as they (Mike and his mother) felt that was the best approach. Mike's dad has never spoken of it to Mike. Mike has merely avoided conflict in what would be a lost battle for sure, and would only further fracture the amicable "don't ask, don't tell" relationship he has with his father. On the second issue, we explained that we would tell children that Mike's dad and brother don't like me and that's why they don't come to visit. When their age is right, then they'll probably work out there is more to it and we'll be able to discuss it. We also made the point that it's *we* who are being assessed, not our relatives. Miranda replied that relatives play a big part, although she had been told by the gay panel Chair that it is not uncommon for gay men and lesbians to be rejected by close relatives.

By the end of the discussion she appeared to be looking for a solution rather than looking for a problem. She asked Mike to write a statement about the stuff we'd talked about and she added that she thought we had a lot to offer to a child and didn't want this to stop us getting through the panel *but* she still fears it might, and she needs more information, will need to speak to her supervisor again, and we will need to discuss it once more at the next interview.

In all we spent nearly another 90 minutes talking about this and by the time Miranda left, three hours after she had arrived, we were exhausted and emotionally drained. We decided to treat ourselves to dinner at our favourite restaurant, which helped us switch off for a bit, but we're at a loss as to how this situation can be resolved. This is the lowest point we have reached so far. It feels like the situation is totally out of our hands and we can't do anything about it other than keep explaining and hope that she eventually understands.

Friday 10th October

We've been a bit numb and generally feeling down for the last few days. We're trying to be positive, but all we keep coming back to is the fact that unless we can make Miranda see that the issues she brought up don't affect our ability to parent, we won't be taken to the panel. We know there are routes we could take if indeed that is the final decision, such as making a complaint, asking for a review, or changing agencies, but at this stage we'd rather not think about that. We're still going on, of course, and haven't lost any of our eagerness to adopt. Maybe we'll look back on this at some point as a good test of our determination. And it may be that that's just what Miranda is doing to a certain extent: testing us.

On the positive side she's clearly still intending for us to continue as we have another two interviews scheduled and we've heard from our referees that they've received letters asking for references. Miranda did say she thought we had a lot to offer, so we're hanging on to that thought.

Friday 17th October

After the last interview we told a few friends about what Miranda had said and how low we were feeling about it. We've had lots of support and everyone keeps telling us that it'll just be a bump along the way and it will sort itself out. After a while we got fed up of discussing it so we've had a few days of trying not to talk about adoption at all. We need to get ready for the next interview, though, so Mike sent Miranda his statement explaining how comfortable he is with his sexuality and the situation with his father. She hasn't replied, so we'll see what she says.

Monday 20th October

Miranda is coming tomorrow and we're nervous as hell. Last night we finished our "homework" in preparation for the interview: our ecomap and a list of how we expect our lives will change if we adopt. But the main thing is not the themes of this particular interview, but her reaction to Mike's statement and whether her supervisor has changed her mind regarding our suitability. We've both been rather tense all day. We're convinced that Miranda is going to say that this is as far as we go, and we have a mixture of feelings that range from sad to angry. We know that there is no reason why she should say "no" (at least that we can see), but after the last interview anything is possible. We don't want this to be the end but we're worried that it may be. The ridiculous thing is how ludicrous the whole argument is. Whilst I understand that it would be great if the children we may adopt had a relationship with their grandfather, at the end of the day if Mike's father had died years ago it would not be an issue. Or don't they approve people who can't provide grandparents? As for Miranda's impression that Mike is not comfortable with his sexuality, God knows where she got that from. I'm sure tomorrow everything will be fine and we'll laugh at how much we've worked ourselves up and what drama queens we've turned into with this whole thing. Or so I hope.

Tuesday 21st October

Miranda came over this morning and the first thing she told us was that she'd met with her supervisor and panel advisor and they were happy for us to proceed. They still think that Mike's dad is an issue, but they acknowledge that the situation is not likely to change. They said that this will come up at the panel, and she is going to make sure that she has all the information she needs, so she will interview those among our referees who know Mike's dad. We were so relieved! We'd worked ourselves up and convinced ourselves that this was it, so to hear something positive was really encouraging and uplifting.

The interview today focused on our reasons for wanting to adopt and how we think our life will change. Miranda seemed quite happy with the lists we had made. We also spoke about schools and activities for kids in our area. As it happens, we are lucky to have lots of activity places near us, so she was quite satisfied with that as well, although she would like us to compile a list for the next interview.

Miranda told us that she's received four of our references so far, including those from our employers. She mentioned that she'll also request references from the places where we volunteer.

Our next interview is not for another three weeks, and that one will focus on our experience of looking after children. It's unfortunate that she is so busy and we have to wait so long between visits. Another couple we know who are with the same adoption team had weekly interviews and are going to the panel next month, but we understand we have to be patient.

Wednesday 5th November
On Monday we went to see the only other male gay couple who've ever adopted in our local authority. Miranda suggested we might like to talk to them, and I got their email address through New Family Social. They welcomed us into their beautiful home, and were happy to discuss their adoption with us, which was really helpful. We also got to meet their lovely daughter. She was so sweet! We chatted about all sorts of things and they were very encouraging and gave us very good advice.

Tuesday 11th November
Mike got his Beaver uniform last week and we stitched his badges on. He looks so cute (but ever so slightly nerdy) in his shirt, necker and woggle!

Today at the nursery, preparations were under way for the Nativity play. The teacher asked the five-year-olds if they knew who was born on Christmas day. The first answer was "Guy Fawkes", followed by "Joseph" (he of the Amazing Technicolor Dreamcoat). She patiently managed to just about set the story straight...

Thursday 13th November

Miranda came yesterday for our fourth joint interview. This one focused on our experience of and with children. We talked about the children we are in contact with (relatives' or friends' children), our volunteer work at the nursery and Beavers, and what we have learnt from it. We also talked about how we were brought up by our parents, and what we would do differently.

It's all moving ahead now! Miranda hopes that we can go to the panel in early February. She thinks we should only need one or two more interviews. There seems to be some light at the end of the tunnel as far as this part of the process is concerned! We are not letting ourselves get too excited though, as she still thinks that Mike's relationship with his father may be a hurdle at the panel.

Thursday 20th November

As part of the preparation for our next interview, we've been going through the list of specific matching considerations in the old "Form F". It's a list of the history and problems that a child may have, and prospective adopters are asked to tick what they would actively seek, consider or reject. The list ranges from the sort of things most adopters would expect, such as "a child who has been abandoned", or "a child who needs to maintain face-to-face contact with birth parent(s)" to more challenging decisions such as "a child with Down's Syndrome", "a child who may display sexualised behaviour towards adults and other children", or "a child born as a result of rape/incest". Obviously, some prospective adopters will feel better prepared for some things than others, but they are still very big decisions to make. It somehow feels really abstract when you don't know to what degree the child will be affected. For example, when ticking "hearing impairment", you may be talking about a child who is deaf in one ear or a completely deaf child, which would present quite different challenges both for the child and their parents. As it happens, the new Prospective Adopter's Report form (PAR) doesn't actually include that list any longer, but Miranda thought it would be helpful for us to go through it anyway.

The decision-making process is not helped by the fact that the more you limit what you are able to take on, the fewer chances you will have of being matched with a child. We all know there aren't any perfect children out there and this has been made very clear to us. Having said this, we both believe that it is very important to be honest and not to tick something just to look good or because we think it may improve our chances of being matched.

Age is the other decision that we will need to make. Initially, I was leaning towards the nought to five age range, and Mike more towards two to eight. The lower range is pretty much a non-starter since we keep being told that as a gay couple it is very unlikely we'll be matched with a child under two.

Wednesday 26th November
Last weekend Mike and I finally completed the specific matching considerations list. We both made our own decisions separately and then put our lists together. Thankfully, they were almost identical, and we easily reached a consensus.

What was most difficult about it was the realisation that everything we've been reading, been told in training or by other adopters, suddenly stops being "theory" and becomes almost a reality. The adoption "journey" takes you from the initial idea when you first make enquiries with a healthy "normal" baby in mind, to the prospect of an older child who has gone through some degree of trauma. The books you read and the training you get help you to come around to this idea. And I think that the key moment when you accept this and let go of your "fantasy child" is when you go through the Form F list. Although we had mentally pictured it, I think emotionally we didn't fully accept it until last weekend.

Of course, you're only ticking that you would consider a child with X, Y or Z, not signing that you definitely will. You're not actually saying "yes" but "maybe". And you may never be faced with the question anyway, which is another thing I find hard to get used to: that this may all be academic, since we don't know whether we'll be approved, if we'll be matched, or what sort of issues the children will come with...In a way, I think I'd rather be told 'You're definitely going to be matched with a child that has this disability or that problem' so we could do our research and be well prepared. Or we may be matched with a child that doesn't present any of the issues that we have ticked. But we know that's not likely, and I think being gay adopters makes that even less likely.

Miranda is coming tomorrow for our next interview and I know it will be emotionally really hard to discuss this. One of the books I am reading has a graph that shows these last stages of the home study as the lowest point in the process. Although I'm fairly sure that there will be harder times to come, I can sort of see where they're coming from. And it is reassuring to see it in black and white. As usual, knowing that other people have been through the same thing helps you to cope.

Thursday 27th November
Miranda came for our fifth interview today. We went

through the "specific matching considerations list" item by item, discussing whether we were a "yes", a "no", or a "limited". As it turns out, we had filled it in wrong. We thought a "yes" meant we were actively seeking children with that particular condition, so we hadn't ticked any, as we are not looking for a child with any special background. But a "yes" just means that you will consider a child, not that you are actively looking. The form says to tick "yes" if you are "positively interested", which is what caused the confusion. Anyhow, this meant that we had to reconsider whether some of our choices were a straight "yes" or "limited" there and then. Thankfully Mike and I were thinking along the same lines.

At one point, we made a comment about how our being a gay couple would probably exclude us from being matched with children who needed to be brought up in certain religions that are very vocal about their opposition to homosexuality. We also mentioned how it might be difficult to get into a Catholic school, and that we wouldn't like teachers to tell our children that being gay is wrong. Miranda just said that she hadn't thought of that as she just sees us as Mike and Pablo, and not "a gay couple".

One thing we were both really pleased with is the fact that, for the first time, Miranda was talking about us being matched with a child as a realistic prospect. Considering how negative she was about us making it to the panel at all only a few weeks ago, it felt really good to hear her talk about it in such a way.

Sunday 30th November

Today a couple who have been friends of ours for a long time came to visit with their two boys, aged six and three. The kids are usually lovely and well-behaved, but for some reason today they weren't. They kept fighting, were difficult with food, moody…We know that this was an "off" day for them and not at all the norm, but as soon as they left we did sigh with relief. Then we looked at each other thinking that if we have our own, no one will take them away after a few hours when they're being difficult, and there won't be any respite.

Monday 1st December

Good news! Both couples who did the preparation course with us have been approved. Rebecca and Alan have had to wait three very stressful weeks for a final decision after their panel couldn't reach a consensus, but the other couple got a straight yes last Friday. Both are heterosexual married couples, so it's not quite the same as our situation, but it's still encouraging and we are really chuffed for them.

Tuesday 2nd December

Miranda came today for our final joint interview. We discussed contact with birth families: how we felt about it and how much contact we would be willing to agree to, what type (letterbox, face-to-face) and with whom (siblings, grandparents, birth parents). We pretty much agreed to anything that the child's social worker considers best at first; then we'll see, depending on how the child reacts and whether it upsets them. Contact is probably the one issue that I have completely changed my mind about after the preparation course and all the books we've been reading. If you had asked me about contact with the birth family a year ago, I'd have been reluctant, but now I can really see how much the children need to stay in touch with siblings and to have some realistic connection to their birth parents, if only to avoid idealised fantasies.

We sorted out some paperwork, and Miranda went through our birth and marriage certificates, pay slips and bank statements to make sure we are who we say we are and to check that we'll be financially stable, especially during any time that we may be on adoption leave.

In the next few days Miranda is going to visit four of our

referees, including Mike's mum. She doesn't get to visit my family, although I'm sure she tried to convince our local authority to pay for a trip to Spain! After that she will finish writing our report, which she hopes to have ready in early January. She's also arranged for another social worker to come in January for our second opinion interview. IF all goes according to plan and there are no delays, we should be ready to go to the panel in February! I'm sure the nerves will kick in soon...

Friday 5th December

Mike and I filled in the forms to have our medicals done. We've read about people getting a bit worried about their medicals, and indeed, as I filled it in I kept wondering if anything in there would not be to the liking of the medical adviser. I think it's unlikely, but of course it's natural to wonder.

I went to the nursery and was asked to help out with the little ones who are either just three or two coming up to three. It was great to have the opportunity to work with younger children. I played games and read stories to them and worked mostly with little Jack, who has a rare syndrome. His face is somewhat disfigured, he can't walk or stand that well unaided, has a hearing aid and has to wear a bib as he drools constantly. His speech is quite hard to understand, but he is so lovely and so bright. It's misleading, because when you first see him you feel pity for him and assume, mostly because of his facial disfigurement, that he is not fully developed cognitively, but he is very clever. I really enjoyed spending time with him, but I have to admit that I wouldn't want to care for him 24/7. In that sense, the fact that adoptive parents can, to a certain extent, choose what physical limitations they are prepared to cope with, is an advantage, as I'm sure Jack's parents did not set out to bring up a child with his condition.

Sunday 7th December

Yesterday we went to the New Family Social gathering. It was the Christmas "do" and the kids and parents had a good time. We caught up with some of the people we had met before, people whose messages we have read online, and also the couple that we visited last month. Once again we came out of the meeting feeling inspired: a welcome shot of optimism.

Wednesday 10th December

Miranda's been interviewing our referees this week. On Monday she went to see one of my oldest friends in this country and today she visited both Mike's mum and his oldest friend. They were all told that anything they said would be confidential, so of course the first thing they all did as soon as she left was to ring us. Their interviews lasted about one hour each and they were asked about how they met us, how long ago, what they think about our plans to adopt, whether they support us, if they think that we are sufficiently prepared...the sort of things they were expecting to be asked. They all reported that they thought the interviews went well. Let's hope Miranda has the same impression!

Wednesday 17th December

We had our medicals today. The first thing my GP said was how ridiculous it is that we had to go through a medical to adopt, when other people can just 'pop them out'. We paid £73.86 each and the secretary asked us if the medicals were for an adoption. We replied that they were and she just said 'Wicked!' This was the first time we've told someone we didn't know at all, and her reaction was just so positive that it felt really good. I've always been concerned about situations like going into shops with our child, for example, where it will be obvious that the two of us are the parents, and how people will react. I realise it won't be like this every time, but for a first reaction it was great.

Tuesday 23rd December

I saw an article in the paper today reporting that many countries are now changing their intercountry adoption policies, explicitly or implicitly, to exclude single and gay adopters. China, Russia, Ukraine, and Belarus now require that adopters be joined in a heterosexual marriage with a high income and even with university degrees in some cases. The article mentions that the only two countries that actually accept gay prospective adopters are Brazil and Burkina Faso. In the case of Brazil, this is only allowed if the child is over six years of age or suffers from a long-term illness or disability. Clearly gay parents are only welcome to take away the children that nobody else wants in those countries.

Yesterday Pope Benedict said that humankind is facing self-destruction and that saving humanity from homosexual or transsexual behaviour was as important as protecting the environment. It's nice of the Catholic Church to send such an inclusive message three days before Christmas, isn't it? As a Catholic myself, do I feel particularly accepted by my church at this time of year?...I don't think so.

Wednesday 24th December

I've been in Spain with my parents for the last five days. Last night all my nieces came to stay. First we had to assign them to different beds. Then one of them decided at the last minute that she didn't actually want to stay any longer and wanted Mummy to pick her up. But Mummy had gone out to dinner and I had to explain, comfort and dry some tears. Then this morning I was woken up by my youngest niece at 5.30. She'd wet the bed so she and it needed changing. Then the eight-year-old and her sister decided to have a fight. I love being an uncle and can't wait to be a dad. And I actually say this with only the slightest hint of sarcasm: I do love it and I can't wait.

As usual, Mike has stayed back in the UK to spend Christmas with his family. We normally spend it apart, Mike in the UK with his parents and me in Spain with my parents, brother, sister, nieces and nephew. It just works out better that way as we cannot really do Christmas Eve in one place and Christmas Day or Boxing Day in another. It's sort of weird that we've never spent Christmas together in 11 years, but we have a little Christmas reunion when I get back, and open our presents. I suppose if, or rather when we adopt, we'll have to figure out a whole different system!

This time last year I wrote, rather naïvely, about the possibility of it being our last Christmas without kids. This year there's a bigger chance if we get approved in February, but of course it may not happen or we may still be waiting for a match, which is the most likely scenario. Still, without getting my hopes up too much, it's fun to imagine what next Christmas with our own children would be like. We might not be able to leave the country for starters, so who knows if we'd manage to see my family. Then if we did, how would all the children get on together and in what language would they communicate? And we'd have to explain that there are no crackers, silly hats, turkey or mince pies in Spain, but you get to eat turrón and seafood instead...

Thursday 25th December
Today, as my nieces and nephew opened presents and I helped to put toys together and played with them, I couldn't help feeling a little bit sad and hoping that in the not too distant future Mike and I have our own child or children staring open-mouthed and wide-eyed at a room full of nicely-wrapped presents, opening them excitedly, and showing them to us as we pretend that we didn't know what was under the tree.

Not so keen on the ensuing fight later about who got to play with what, whether one of them had really stepped on a toy on purpose, and who'd had the last piece of jigsaw that was missing...but I'm glossing over that bit.

4

2009

Wednesday 7th January

I emailed Miranda yesterday with a little reminder that we were supposed to finalise the home study this week with the "second opinion" visit from one of her colleagues. She rang a bit later to tell me that she was planning to have our report ready next week and hoped to arrange the second opinion interview to coincide with that. We had told her that Mike would be away on a work trip next week, but she'd forgotten. The deadline to submit the documentation in time for the February panel is next Friday, so she's going to find out whether it is possible to delay things slightly. Miranda knows we can't make the next available panel in March as we'll be on holiday. She mentioned that she could always go to the panel without us, but we'd prefer to be there and wait until April if necessary. It's important to us to be able to make our case or answer any questions that may arise, and for the panel to see us to avoid any preconceptions they may have about us. So either Miranda rushes the paperwork, which isn't great, or we have to wait a further two months, which we'd rather not. We could cancel the holiday, but with our luck, something else would probably come up to delay the panel anyway.

Friday 9th January
Miranda rang earlier today. She and her colleague will come on the 19th. The plan is for Miranda to send us our home study report next Friday so we can read it over the weekend and feed back to her when they visit. Her colleague will then write her report on Monday evening or Tuesday morning so that it's all ready. One possible delay could be that, once the report is finished and before it goes to the panel members, it has to be read by Miranda's supervisor. If she requests major changes or wants further evidence of anything, then it probably won't be done in time for us to go to the panel in February. It all feels a bit rushed and we hope that doesn't have a negative effect on the outcome, but after so many months it's very exciting that the home study is finally coming to an end and we could be going to the panel in a month's time!

Sunday 11th January
We had some very good news yesterday. Two guys we met at the June New Family Social meeting have been matched with a seventeen-month-old boy. It's only taken six months from being approved to being matched, which is really fast! We were surprised to hear how young the boy is, as we were told by our local authority that gay couples are never matched with young children. Or is that their own policy?

Saturday 17th January
Yesterday was the deadline for Miranda to send us the home study report. She rang me at work at lunchtime to tell me that she hadn't finished it partly because of a problem with her PC and the report template. She's also been really busy with an assignment for a course she is taking. This means that they won't be coming on Monday to finalise the home study and we won't be going to the panel in February.

She apologised three times and once again offered to go to the panel without us in March, but we want to be there. That means that we're now looking at April.

Miranda said that another reason she thought it best to take time with the report was the fact that she still thinks there is an issue with Mike's father, and she wants to make sure she is happy with how that is explained in the report.

Mike is not surprised, as he never thought that everything would get done in time, but I had actually hoped that we could get the approval out of the way, especially knowing that it could take months – if not years – to be matched. So while we realise that in the big scheme of things this is not a huge setback, we are really disappointed.

Monday 19th January
At the weekend we met up with Jonathan and Stuart, two guys we met through New Family Social, who live near us and adopted a six-year-old boy last year. Their son is a very sociable chatty boy who was happy to talk to us, show us his toys and even the book that his dads made for him just before they were introduced. They must have answered a thousand questions for us. They've not had any problems at school with the other kids or their parents, which is something that has always worried us. Their son has really settled with them now and it's a pleasure to see them together as they make a great family. After such a disappointing start to the weekend, it was great to spend the afternoon with them.

Wednesday 28th January
We had hoped that Miranda would have got back to us by now with dates for the home study report and the second opinion interview, but we've heard nothing from her. We don't want to push her so we are waiting as patiently as we can.

We're continuing with our reading. Mike's reading *The Primal Wound* and I am reading *Building the Bonds of Attachment: Awakening love in deeply troubled children*. They don't make for easy reading...

Thursday 29th January

Yesterday, the *Daily Mail* published a story about how the parents of a heroin addict were not allowed to look after their grandchildren when they were taken into care, and the children are now going to be placed with a gay couple. The paper called it 'a sickening assault on family life'. The reporting ignores why the children can't stay with their grandparents, for which there must be very good reasons. Today it was followed up by another article, which we read on their website. The article was bad, but worse are the comments their readers post online, many of which start with: 'I'm not a homophobe BUT...' and go on with utterly homophobic comments. I actually wept when I read them. Just when you think that you live in a world that may accept you, it's heartbreaking.

Friday 30th January

We've heard from Miranda. She's been working on our report and she'll be in touch soon.

Monday 2nd February

Yet another article about gay adoption in the *Daily Mail*. Last Friday, a *Daily Mail* journalist wrote about how we "gays" have been shown tolerance and respond with tyranny.

The whole thing has been incredible. Mike and I have been through a rollercoaster of emotions. After initial outrage, we were sad about the case and the consequences it may have for the couple involved (and the children, of course) and also our own situation. People on the gay adoption messageboards have reported a shift in attitude among co-workers and other people they know. After the sadness, though, we wondered, 'What are we doing?', 'Could this happen to us?' And we even had some doubts about whether what we are doing is right for the children. Things looked up when we read the beautiful message that one of the New Family Social members posted on the messageboard reassuring everyone that we are doing the right thing, and highlighting her very positive experience as an adopter. She is absolutely right, of course.

In a way, I think that the issue of gay adoption and the effect it may have on children is similar to how children from minority ethnic origins who grow up in a predominantly white environment may be affected. Those parents will need to prepare their children for racism just as we will need to prepare our children for homophobia.

Thursday 5th February
Miranda rang yesterday. It turns out that she needs a Spanish Criminal Records Bureau check for me, which she hadn't mentioned before. Considering that until a few weeks ago we were supposed to be going to the panel tomorrow, it seems quite an oversight, but maybe they don't assess that many foreigners in our local authority. As it happens I will be in Spain next week, so I hope to be able to get it done while I'm there. Also, their medical adviser has returned our medical reports and they are fine – well, fine-ish. There aren't any major issues, but Mike's body mass index is just over 30, so they have suggested that he loses some weight. He's not impressed. Just how perfect do they expect adopters to be?

Miranda also said that she had some more questions for us, but she would just email them. They deal once again with Mike's father, and there are some follow-up questions on the personalities of the children we would be interested in. She also asks about whether we've ever been bullied because of our sexuality, and how we would deal with any bullying a child might suffer because of having gay dads. I wonder if this latter question has been prompted by recent media coverage of gay adoption...

In any case, we have set up a meeting in just under three weeks to discuss our home study report so we assume we'll receive it before then. It looks like things are moving again!

Friday 6th February
We sent the replies to Miranda's queries today and she was happy with them, but later rang and asked a couple more questions. In her defence, she had warned us from the beginning that, because this would be the first time she was using the new Prospective Adopter's Report form that's replaced the old "Form F", she might have extra little bits to ask as she goes through it. We're not complaining as it means she's obviously working on our report.

The questions this time were about how "Spanish" our household is. We told her that we don't speak Spanish in the house. Mike has done a few courses and gets by, but is not fluent, but we do have some traditions such as celebrating Epiphany and my saint's day: mine is on 29th June but we don't celebrate Mike's saint's day – he claims that he is Saint Mike for putting up with me, but that's another story. We also mentioned that we cook Spanish food often and I sometimes watch Spanish TV on Sky and listen to Spanish music. I'm not sure if this means that we get "bonus points" if there are any Spanish children out there, or that we are excluded if children do not match our origins. I was going to write "ethnic origin" but it seems a bit silly considering that I am white European, just like any Brit – in fact Mike looks more Mediterranean than I do! I sincerely hope that our varied background opens doors rather than closes them.

Tuesday 10th February
I'm back in Spain for a few days and yesterday I managed to sort out my Spanish Criminal Record Check. Glad to

report it's all clear.

Thursday 12th February

I was walking down the street in my home town here in Spain today when I saw a small poster stuck to an advertising display. The poster shows a gay and a lesbian couple, both with children. The text reads: 'Who are these people? No. I want a normal family.' Underneath it is the web address for the National Alliance and their slogan: 'Defending the family'.

So yes, Spain may have same-sex marriage and allow gay adoption, but it also has a political party that actually spends money producing these posters and sticking them to our walls for everyone to see. Alas, we're not their only target. In fact anyone who isn't white, Catholic, and born in Spain is a target. Thankfully they are a minority and as far as I know have never won any seats in any local or national elections.

Friday 20th February

I've been back in the UK for a week, but we took a few days off straight after I got back from Spain. It was nice to be off together, even in cold weather. There were children on half-term everywhere, and all of the places we visited had activities for kids, which made us realise that we could have done pretty much the same stuff if we had children with us.

Miranda rang once more to ask Mike some questions about his family tree and we've now got dates for our final interview with her to go through her report: Monday afternoon! She was hoping to post it so we could read it beforehand, but if not, we will have to read it and comment on the spot, which I'm not so keen on as I'd prefer to have time to digest it. It may arrive tomorrow or Monday morning, but based on past performance we're thinking it won't. Then on Wednesday we will have our second opinion interview. And then...that'll be it! Panel next.

Sunday 22nd February

We had hoped that we'd get to see the report before we have our final interview with Miranda tomorrow, but nothing arrived in the post yesterday, which means we'll have to read it in front of her.

Monday 23rd February

Miranda came just before four and she was here for three hours. She had some "leftover" questions for the Prospective Adopter's Report and more questions that the panel adviser had asked. Some of these were once again about Mike's father and about how we would address any homophobic bullying our children might encounter. Then she asked us to do a little exercise: we each had to write on separate pieces of paper how we imagined a moment on any given day after we had adopted. How many children, ages, sex, type of activity we'd be doing...Then she gave us a copy of the report each and we sat there reading it under her watchful eye. This was a bit unnerving as it felt like a timed comprehension exercise at school! We only had small comments to make regarding spellings and dates, and some phrasing. Miranda will send the full report once she has added the answers to all the questions she asked today and we will get a chance to read it all again and make comments. She is hoping to do this by Friday at the latest.

Monday 2nd March

Miranda popped round to drop off the final version of the report on Friday afternoon. It's a whopping 72 pages: 46 for the main report and the rest for appendices and additional forms. There are still a couple of spelling and minor errors with names and ages and stuff like that, but it's all there. I am actually quite amazed at how well Miranda has got to know us in the last few months over the course of one individual interview with each of us and seven joint sessions. Her facts are accurate and her reflections very encouraging. Hopefully, she will convey that to the panel and get us approved. She's postponed the date for an operation because she didn't want to be responsible for us having to delay our panel date again. That's incredibly nice of her.

On Friday she also lent us a children's book on dealing with racism. She thinks it will help us deal with homophobic bullying. She has also lent us the BAAF guide *Recruiting, Assessing and Supporting Lesbian and Gay Carers and Adopters*. It looks like it will be a very useful book. If nothing else, at least to get an idea of what training panel members and social workers may have received to help them deal with gay and lesbian couples.

Tuesday 3rd March

Miranda and the "second opinion social worker" visited us today. This other social worker was actually one of the two who did our initial interview back in January last year, but we hadn't seen her since. She asked us some questions, starting with Mike's relationship with his father, which we had to explain for the umpteenth time, and then asked about the number and sex of children we are hoping for. She talked about the uncertainties that surround many of the children in the care system. We also discussed prejudice and contact. They were the kinds of questions that she expects the panel may ask us. Both she and Miranda seem quite positive about us being approved, but she said that if we do get approved, we should get ready for a long wait, given that in some social workers' minds gay couples are near the bottom of the pecking order after heterosexual couples and single women. I couldn't help wondering: is that in "some" social workers' minds or her own?

The interview lasted just over an hour and a quarter and after they had gone we were completely drained and unsure about the end of the assessment process. It's suddenly all very real, and for the first time we're allowing ourselves to believe that we may actually get approved. I think perhaps we've been expecting a hurdle that we wouldn't be able to overcome. And now all that's left is to see whether the panel agrees with the social workers' assessment.

It's a month until we go to the panel and the work is done, so all we can do is wait. In the meantime we're going on holiday for two weeks. When we were planning it, we kept thinking this may be our last major holiday before we adopt, but given the comment we heard today about getting ready to wait a long time, it may not be so.

Friday 20th March
We're back from our holiday. We had a lovely time and managed to relax and switch off for a whole two weeks, which doesn't happen often! Well, we did talk about the adoption a few times.

We were supposed to receive the report from the second opinion interview before we left, but it didn't arrive on time and we had to find an internet café while we were away. The report was quite positive overall, although once again it made a big deal of Mike's relationship with his dad. We just don't know any more if this will turn out to be nothing at all or our stumbling block, but as there is nothing more we can do about it, we'll just have to wait and see. If there are any questions about it at the panel we will try to explain as best as we can. What was a little puzzling was the fact that the report referred to us as "the two men", which seemed to be making an issue of our sexuality. It could have said "the couple" or "Mike and Pablo", "the applicants"...I don't know, it sounded strange.

We also had an email from Miranda to say that she is having the operation she'd delayed so she could complete our report; she is actually on sick leave right now and won't be back to work until three days before the panel. Hopefully, all will be well, she'll recover in time, and there won't be any further delays!

Tuesday 24th March
The Home Office in Morocco has decided to threaten publications that defend homosexuality or portray it in a positive light after a magazine published a story about an unofficial gay wedding. Homosexuality is criminalised in Morocco.

When we have a moan about the slow adoption process, or encounter homophobia from social workers or authorities, we forget just how privileged we are to live in enlightened places where gay adoption is allowed at all. No matter how convinced we are that we can make good parents and offer a child a loving home, there are many places in the world where that is not an option and we should count our blessings, even if the system is not perfect.

Thursday 26th March
The main character in the novel I'm currently reading (*The Miracle at Speedy Motors* by Alexander McCall Smith) adopts two orphans, and, in one chapter, the adopted boy is struggling with his identity and with the fact that he is adopted. After reassuring him, the parent realises that she has now come to the point where she considers herself his mother and thinks: 'We could all be a mother, all of us; even a man could be a mother.'

I loved that line. Even though it's not about gay adoption, the implication is that a man can do just as good a job as a woman in raising children. I think many people's prejudices about gay men adopting are not necessarily about the gay bit, although there are plenty who have a problem with that, but about men in general adopting. I have personally never encountered among my friends and acquaintances any reservations about us adopting because we are gay (at least to our faces), but on a couple of occasions people have expressed quite sexist opinions, like 'a child needs a mum'. I think this is one of those areas where adoption differs for gay men and lesbians: being raised without a father is acceptable; plenty of single mothers out there to prove the point, but being raised without a mother can be perceived as unfair on the children, or at least putting them at a disadvantage.

Saturday 28th March

Yesterday we had dinner with our small local prospective adopters' group, Gavin and Sue, and Rebecca and Alan. Gavin and Sue have identified two sets of children they are interested in and their social worker agrees that they would be a good match, so she is going to get in touch with their respective social workers to arrange visits if possible. There is even better news for Rebecca and Alan: they are going to the matching panel next week! We are so pleased for them. They will actually go to the panel just before us, so we will probably see them on the day.

Today we've received the letter from our local authority confirming the time of our panel, giving us directions, and asking us to reply confirming that we would like to attend. We were under the impression that we would get a list of the panel members but we haven't. We may ask about that, as it would be good to know who we'll be facing.

Tuesday 31st March

The letter from our local authority with the information about the panel members arrived today. We also got a phone call from Miranda, who is back at work. I mentioned that we were a little concerned when we read that the panel Chair works for a Catholic adoption agency, as we fear she may not be too keen on adoption by gay men, but Miranda says that she's worked with her before and she thinks it won't be an issue. She suggested we read some of the information we sent her, so that it's fresh in our minds, especially the statement Mike sent her regarding his relationship with his father. She also suggested that on

Friday I let Mike answer questions first, otherwise he won't get a word in edgeways! The cheek! She's right, of course.

Thursday 2nd April

The panel's tomorrow and we've managed to survive the week without getting too anxious. Tomorrow will be another story, of course. What's weird is thinking that tomorrow is likely to be one of the most significant days of our lives, whatever the outcome.

So what if it's a "no"? We don't really want to think about that too much, but we need to consider that we may be rejected at the panel. The obvious thing to do would be to contest the decision through the Independent Review Mechanism. Failing that, we could go to another agency I suppose (if an agency will take us after being turned down). It would depend on what reasons we are given to justify the rejection.

Friday 3rd April

Last night Mike was uncharacteristically nervous. He's normally the quiet one and I am the one who gets fidgety, but I was really calm. Possibly to compensate for Mike's nerves. We read some of the stuff we'd written during the home study and then prepared answers to questions Miranda had suggested we might be asked. The big question was how we might explain Mike's relationship with his dad to a child in our care. We came up with good points to make, but Mike was really uncomfortable and tense. He told me that he was sure that we were going to be turned down and it would be his fault. He was certain that the problem with his father was going to be the one we could not overcome and felt responsible for it. I reminded him that he is not responsible for his father's actions.

When we woke up we turned on the news and heard that Madonna's adoption attempt in Malawi had failed. Was it an omen? Was today a day for failed adoption dreams? We drove 40 minutes down to the place where the local authority panel meets. On the way I read out text messages and emails from friends. It was really sweet to feel the support from everyone; it meant a lot.

We arrived just after eleven. Rebecca and Alan were there, waiting to hear the outcome of their matching panel. We said a quick "hello" and were then ushered to the far side of the room to give them some privacy. We saw the panel Chair approach them and then their smiles. They came over to us as soon as she left and told us they've been matched with a nine-month-old little girl. They were glowing with happiness. We were delighted for them.

Miranda arrived. She said that she'd been over the paperwork again last night and was feeling confident, even though she didn't look it. The panel Chair came to introduce herself and explained they would first start the meeting with Miranda and then she, the Chair, would come to get us. They went up to the panel room at 11.15 and we sat and waited. We had another look at the notes we'd prepared last night. Mike spilled his coffee three times, although thankfully he managed to avoid spilling it all over himself.

The Chair came down at 12.10 to fetch us. We made our way up the stairs and entered the room. For some reason I had pictured it as some sort of courtroom, but it just had a large table with lots of people sitting round it. All the panel members had printed cards in front of them with their names and their roles. They each introduced themselves in turn. There were about 10 members: Chair, medical adviser, social workers, adopters acting as independent members, a guy from a psychiatric service, an administrator, and an observer as well as the panel adviser from our local authority and Miranda. Most of them were smiling, so it didn't feel too threatening.

The Chair listed what they thought our strengths were: our very stable relationship, support network, excellent references and our voluntary work. She then asked us how we'd found the assessment and to identify one thing that had stood out in the learning process. We said how we'd found the process less intrusive than we'd expected and how we'd probably never have considered contact with birth families before the preparation course, and now understood why it is so important. After that she asked Mike about his working pattern, and whether he'd have to spend many nights away from home. Mike replied that he hardly ever has to be away because of his job any more, as it's changed recently and many things can be done online.

The next question was about our marital status. They were a bit confused by the fact that we were married in Spain and how that "translated" under UK law. Mike replied that 'the marriage means nothing', and I had to step in to explain that what he meant was that it wasn't recognised as a marriage under UK law but it was recognised as a civil partnership. Everyone laughed at Mike's wording, which helped to break the ice a bit. Then we were asked if we had a preference for boys or girls. We explained that most of the parents in our support network have boys and of course we feel somewhat better prepared for boys having been boys ourselves. We added that it has been pointed out to us that gay men tend to be matched with boys.

Next we were asked about female role models. We mentioned the names of females in our support network, which will include the parents of the children that any child of ours meets at school or at other activities. Finally, we were asked about other gay parents we had met, and whether they had encountered any negative reactions. We talked about New Family Social members and in particular about Jonathan and Stuart, and how they hadn't experienced any problems with other children, their parents, or the teachers at their boy's school.

While we spoke most members were nodding and

smiling and we weren't made to feel uncomfortable at all, although one of the members looked quite stern.

After about 15 minutes of questions, we were asked to wait downstairs while they discussed their decision. As soon as we got downstairs we both commented that we'd not been asked about Mike's father at all. After all the preparation for that particular question and the times it had been stressed to us that that could be the biggest hurdle for the panel! We decided that either they were so clear that they weren't going to approve us that it wasn't worth bothering to go that way, or Miranda really had done her job at explaining the situation.

Ten minutes after we'd left the room Miranda and the Chair came down. Miranda was quite poker-faced, so I did fear the worst for a moment, but the Chair said, 'You can smile now,' and then she told us how pleased she was to say that we'd been unanimously recommended for approval. We were both so relieved! She told us that because of Easter it may be a while before we get the letter of approval from the decision maker (who has to write to us within five working days) but she said that the outcome was unlikely to be any different from the panel's recommendation given that their decision had been unanimous.

Once the Chair had left, Miranda told us that the panel thought that Mike's relationship with his father and brother was something that an adopted child could relate to, as is the fact that I have mild dyslexic tendencies, and that I was bullied at school.

We got in the car and texted everyone. The first reply came from Mike's mum and that made us quite emotional. All the way home we got lots of lovely texts from friends and family. I was reading them to Mike, who was driving, and my voice kept shaking as I read them out.

The phone hasn't stopped ringing. We've booked a table at our favourite restaurant and we'll be having a quiet celebration, just the two of us. Tomorrow we're seeing some of our friends and we'll have a bigger one. This has been a day we'll never forget.

Sunday 5th April
A friend has alerted us to another *Daily Mail* story. This time it's about two brothers who are being adopted by a gay couple. The *Daily Mail* reports the concerns of the birth family that a gay couple will not provide a stable environment and that their children will learn to do such things as holding hands with other boys. And they add that it's against the birth family's Christian values.

The article makes it seem as if children were being taken away from their parents to fill some imaginary quota of gay adoptions. It would be funny if it wasn't so serious. Their readers actually believe what these people write.

Reading the article got us down. It spoilt the wonderful mood we'd been in since the panel. I feel so sorry for the couple concerned. They've been matched with those children and one of the most memorable moments of their life is being ruined.

Tuesday 7th April
Miranda rang today to let us know that the department's decision maker has confirmed the panel's recommendation and we are now approved for one or two children, aged between nought and seven. They could be one boy, two boys or a boy and girl sibling group, but not one or two girls. No idea why this is and she couldn't explain either.

In the meantime, the biggest consequence is that we can make decisions again! We know that being approved doesn't mean that we will be matched with a child or that we will definitely adopt, but we are being positive and assuming that it will happen. This means that we no longer have to have hypothetical discussions that start with 'if we're approved...' On Friday afternoon we rang the builder to confirm we'll be going ahead with our planned loft conversion to make more room in the house. It isn't terribly big, so it will increase our options to be matched with more than one child. And if we don't get matched, we'll have lots of spare room in the house! We've been saving for a while for this and the bank has agreed to extend our mortgage, so hopefully we'll be able to afford it...

We've had lots more phone calls, emails and texts from family and friends. The common theme (apart from the obvious congratulations) is the same piece of advice: go out and do everything you ever meant to do, because once you have children you'll never go out again!

Monday 13th April
The letter from our local authority confirming our approval arrived last Wednesday. We were happy to see it in black and white. Although it's felt like forever and quite drawn out, a year from the preparation course to being approved doesn't seem that long when you think about it. When you compare us to the two heterosexual couples we met, it's not so different either. We did take a month or so to make up our minds, and there was that break during the summer when I was working away. At the end of the day, what matters is that we are approved now.

I used to worry that Mike wasn't as keen on adopting as I was, but his reaction when the letter confirming our approval arrived was a picture. He was so happy and excited. We were both expecting that after being approved we'd have an 'Oh my God, what have we done?' moment, but that hasn't happened – which is not to say it won't happen at some point...Of course we are now really looking forward to what lies ahead, but this is a life-changing matter and it would be wrong not to wonder whether we really are prepared for something so major and so full of uncertainties.

Thursday 16th April
Miranda rang last week to ask for the dates of the loft conversion, so I emailed them to her yesterday. She says that doing the conversion may mean a delay in starting to look for a match. It should be OK, though, as the work's starting soon and should be finished in June.

Friday 17th April
We met Rebecca and Alan for drinks. They showed us pictures and video clips of their little girl. They started introductions last week and their daughter should move in permanently this Wednesday. They told us everything they could about the linking, matching and introductions (some of it is obviously confidential) and they showed us the room they've got ready and decorated in two weeks. They were beaming; everything seems to be going really well.

One thing that surprises me is that we are genuinely happy for them. This may sound awful, but I feared that when one of the couples from the course was matched we might feel envious. Happily, that hasn't been the case. We've only been approved for just over two weeks, though. If we'd been waiting for several months it might be a different story.

Wednesday 22nd April
The only gay couple to be approved by our local authority before us, whom we met last November, came over for coffee yesterday and brought their lovely daughter with them. She has really grown since we last saw them.

We caught up with her dads and talked about what we've all been up to. They asked us if we were still intending to go for two children and whether we had thought some more about whether we'd prefer boys or girls. A lot of friends have been asking about this since we were approved. We said that in principle we still want two. We know that many people begin with the idea of adopting two children, but then decide to start with one, see how that works, and then maybe go for the second one later. I can see the point. A child who's been in the care system requires therapeutic parenting and a lot of time and patience, so most people would agree that one at a time is more than enough. However, we do like the idea of having two. Two children growing up together learn to share and to understand others' needs. They always have someone else to play – or fight – with and someone else at school who will look out for them. Of course we could adopt one and then another, but if a child is going to have a brother or sister, it may as well be their actual sibling. Then there is always the possibility that if you adopt one child, their birth mother may have another one, but that may or may not happen, and I don't really want to hope that a mother who has had a child removed has another just for our benefit. I think we'll have to play this one by ear. If the right child comes along, we're certainly not going to turn him down just because he hasn't got a sibling.

Sunday 26th April
I've been considering a work trip for October and wasn't sure whether to go ahead with planning it or not. I didn't want to arrange the whole thing, book tickets and hotels and then have to say, 'Sorry, I can't go because I'm going on adoption leave'. But I also don't want to let our lives, in and outside work, grind to a halt based on the possibility that there may be a child for us. So I rang Miranda to ask if she thought it would be OK to book the trip. Her response was 'I wouldn't do it'. She said that as long as we're still considering two children, we may have a shorter wait. October is six months away, and she thought that left quite a gap for things to happen. We don't know how to take her reply. Is she planning something and not telling us? We find the possibility both exciting and scary! Of course, if come October we're still waiting, I'll be most unimpressed.

Mike spent Saturday on a Beavers training course. He's going to become a Beaver leader! The current leader is leaving, and he's been asked to take her place.

Tuesday 5th May
It's such an anticlimax at the moment. After all the excitement and nerves of a month ago, it's strange not to have an interview scheduled or a piece of "homework" to prepare.

It was our second wedding anniversary yesterday so we went out to dinner to celebrate. It was another of those moments when we wondered whether this time next year we'll be celebrating the anniversary with more members in our little family!

Tuesday 12th May
Last week we received new issues of *Children who Wait* and *Be My Parent*. *Be My Parent* has several features this month on same-sex adoption, as well as an article on New Family Social. One of the publications had details of a sibling group we could be interested in. We really shouldn't be "childspotting" (the term I use to try and desensitise myself) in the magazines as we're tied to our local authority for another two months, but after talking about it and reading the details a few times, we have decided to contact Miranda anyway to see what she thinks.

Wednesday 13th May
I emailed Miranda about the sibling group we spotted. She agreed that they 'look like a possibility' but added that they are still hoping to match us with a child from the local authority, and therefore we 'will have to be patient a little longer'. Of course this sent us into a frenzy of trying to second-guess what she means and to read between lines. Is she just saying that we need to be patient because we're still tied to them for another two months and that's all? Or is

she doing some work towards a match that she can't tell us about yet? It's probably the former, but we can't help wondering whether it's the latter.

Thursday 14th May

A letter from the Press Complaints Commission arrived in the post yesterday. Mike wrote to them following the anti-gay adoption articles in early April arguing that the *Daily Mail* had implied that the children in question had been taken away from their mother for the purpose of being placed with a gay couple. They wrote to explain that they had assessed his complaint and decided that there was no breach of the Code of Practice. They say it's regrettable that the distinction between the reasons for removing and placing a child had not been made clearer, but they didn't think that what the *Daily Mail* had printed was likely to mislead its readers. Mike was furious.

Thursday 21st May

Yesterday afternoon we went to see Rebecca and met her and Alan's adopted daughter. She seems to have really settled and Rebecca is already attuned to her daughter's different ways of expressing herself and is clearly head over heels about her. Mike and I played with the baby for a while and she was very responsive. I expected her to start crying the moment we picked her up but she was happy to play with Mike for a good ten minutes before she started reaching for mum. When it was my turn to hold her, she was quite contented, even when her mum left the room to sort out her food. It's heart-warming and encouraging to see such a successful match.

Saturday 30th May

Miranda rang yesterday. She'd like to visit us in two or three weeks' time, when the work in the house is done. That way she can have a look at the loft conversion. Maybe she'll have something to report?

Wednesday 3rd June

It's two months since we were approved. It seems sooo long ago. We were warned that it could be a long wait, but we know of cases where it wasn't and you can't help hoping your case is going to be one of those. In one more month we'll be able to go on the Adoption Register, so our net of possible matches will widen. Until then, we'll keep ourselves busy with the house improvements, voluntary work and more reading.

Friday 5th June

This month's issue of *Be My Parent* arrived today and the siblings we were interested in are no longer featured. I've got really mixed feelings about the fact that they're "gone". You see some kids who appear in the magazines month after month and clearly no one's interested for one reason or another. So I'm happy that they're no longer there because hopefully it means that a family has been found for them. But at the same time I am disappointed that we can't now be considered as a possible match. Is that selfish? I guess it is, and I feel bad about it.

Thursday 11th June

I turned a year older this week. Special dates, like birthdays or Christmas, always make me reassess where I am in terms of achievements during the year that's passed. This time last year we had just been to our first New Family Social meet-up and confirmed with our local authority that we wanted to go ahead with our application to adopt. Looking back, a lot has happened: we went through the ups and downs of the home study and then the approval panel. We've also met some great prospective adopters, adopters, and their kids. It's good to look back and realise that we have moved on. With so little happening in the last two months, it's easy to forget how far we've got in "just" one year. Although looking at it from another angle, some of the couples from our preparation course have now been linked or matched with a child.

Friday 12th June

The Malawi High Court has overturned the previous court ruling and Madonna has been granted the right to adopt for the second time. Good for her. There's been some ridiculous press about "buying babies" and "publicity stunts". As if someone would agree to look after a child for the rest of their lives just for the sake of publicity. If I had her money and position I would use them to speed up our own adoption process too!

Saturday 27th June

The Times reports today on a poll of public attitudes towards gay people. Apparently Britain is a lot more tolerant now than in the past, but there is still a sizeable minority that remains hostile. Adoption seems to be the topic that people are less open-minded about. Even though 68 per cent of those surveyed believe that gay couples should have the same rights as heterosexual couples, only 49 per cent actually agree that we should have the same rights when it comes to adoption.

Sunday 28th June

The last week has brought a lot of happy news for some of the prospective adopters we have met. Gavin and Sue are now the only couple being considered for a sibling group and are waiting to meet their social workers next week, and one of the gay couples we met through New Family Social has been matched with a very cute eighteen-month-old baby boy. We're really pleased for everyone and maybe we'll be where they are in a few months' time. It's fairly clear that not a lot tends to happen in the summer, so we're not hopeful that we'll hear anything before September now.

Friday 10th July

Someone sent me a link to a YouTube video of an advert by a gay rights association. In it, a young man "comes out" as heterosexual to his two dads, who look disappointed. It ends with the slogan 'Children raised by homosexuals do not necessarily become homosexuals'.

I thought it was funny as a reverse take on a gay person coming out to their heterosexual parents. Then I started to think about it and I decided I wasn't keen on the parents' reaction, as the disappointed look makes it seem as though gay people expect their children to be gay too.

I hope my children will grow up in an environment where they'll learn to be open-minded about sexuality, but that shouldn't make them any more or less likely to become gay. In fact, I would much prefer it if they weren't gay. Coming out is very hard, and adopted children go through a difficult enough adolescence. I would rather they didn't have to cope with being gay as well, although I would, of course, support them, and at least they wouldn't have to worry too much about our reaction. Moreover, I would really like to prove wrong all those people who oppose gay adoptions because they think we will turn our children gay!

Monday 13th July

Mike spent Sunday morning taking the Beavers to the local church service and today I went to the nursery for the last time until September. I shall miss the kids during the summer.

It looks like the prospective match for our friends Gavin and Sue is going ahead, although they probably won't be going to the matching panel until September.

Monday 20th July

Miranda came to see us last Friday and liked the loft

conversion. Now that it's been three months since we were approved, and we're no longer tied to our local authority, she has added us to the Adoption Register. She says that our local authority has so few adopters that they'd rather not lose us, though. We're not really sure how to read that. On the one hand, we'll have a better chance with our own local authority as they only have a few adopters. On the other hand, if Miranda is not keen on linking us with children from other authorities, it means we will be considered for fewer children. She said that she hasn't yet written up our profile for other authorities, but she'll draft one and then send it to us for checking.

She mentioned that among the possible children coming up for adoption in our authority are a fourteen-month-old girl and two different one-year-old boys, and she'd like us to be considered for one of them. This caught us by surprise as we have always been told how unlikely it was that we would get a baby or toddler, so we've slowly been coming around to the idea of older children. Also we thought that as we've agreed to consider taking two children, they'd prefer us to go for two, who are normally harder to place. Lots to think about...

Tuesday 4th August

I emailed Miranda last week to ask if she could give us more details about the two one-year-olds she mentioned when she came to see us. She replied that she was only talking about possibilities for the future so we wouldn't get too frustrated that nothing was happening. They are not currently family finding for either child and we shouldn't get too excited. We're not entirely sure how mentioning children that they're not family finding for stops us from being frustrated, but never mind; the outcome is that we're not currently being considered for any children, although Miranda is preparing our profile to send to other local authorities. She will come to see us again in September.

Wednesday 5th August

We had some terrible news from our friends Gavin and Sue. They'd been linked to a sibling group of three children, but last week, when the local authority applied for a placement order to allow the adoption to proceed, the judge decided that he wants to exhaust the possibilities of keeping the children within the birth family. The decision will be reviewed again in a few months' time but until then they will remain in care.

Mike and I were so sorry to hear their news. Sometimes you see similar stories on the online forums or in magazines and although it's always in the back of your mind that it can happen, you desperately hope it won't happen to you or anyone you know. We've always been told that it's all about the children and what's best for them. Whilst I agree that, whenever possible, children should remain within their birth family, it's absolutely ridiculous that no one has the guts to say 'these parents have been given enough opportunities and enough is enough'. The most mind-boggling thing is that, if anyone has any sense, the likely eventual outcome will anyway be a placement order. In the meantime, they'll have spent even more time in care and couples like Gavin and Sue will have been disappointed. I say disappointed but of course the word doesn't even begin to describe how they must feel. The way they spoke about the children made it obvious how "attached" they had become to them already and how much they were looking forward to a quick resolution so their family life together could begin. It must be shattering.

Thursday 6th August

Miranda emailed today to say that she won't be doing our profile until she comes back from her holiday. Many social workers go on holiday in August and she thinks it may get lost among their paperwork when they get back, so she'll do it at the end of the month. So basically that's that for the summer.

Tuesday 11th August
Way back when the *Daily Mail* kicked off with its articles against gay adoption, I wrote to the director of Adoption UK to express my concern about the lack of an "official" response from him. Last June I received an email from their magazine editor asking me to write a piece giving my point of view for *Adoption Today*. Well, they've published it (under pseudonym)! I hope it helps other people to understand how gay adopters and prospective adopters are affected by the spread of prejudice that follows negative publicity.

Also in the same issue, there was an item about a conference called 'Sharing evidence, overcoming resistance: celebrating the role of lesbian and gay carers'. During the conference, the prejudice of children's social workers was highlighted by the speakers, who reported comments such as 'They would prefer the child to go to a normal family'.

On the positive side, there were reports from some studies that showed that:

a) there was no difference in the quality of the relationship between parents and grown-up children brought up in homosexual or heterosexual households;

b) most children brought up by gay or lesbian parents identify themselves as heterosexual;

c) children brought up by gay or lesbian parents are more likely to be teased about their own sexuality during adolescence, but aren't more likely to be teased overall. That is, they may get bullied anyway, only the "theme" of the bullying is likely to be their sexuality. So it's our jobs as parents to prepare them for that.

Also, today I read an article about a special edition of the academic journal, *Adoption Quarterly*, where a study reports that there aren't any significant emotional differences between children brought up by adoptive heterosexual parents and gay parents.

It's really good to read these things. We don't want our sexuality to be a source of difficulties for children we adopt. They'll have enough to cope with as it is!

Wednesday 2nd September

I called the Adoption Register for England and Wales helpline today and they confirmed that we are now on the Register. The woman I spoke to was very helpful and told me the date our names were added (that'll be three days *after* Miranda told us she had added our names, hmmmm...). She also told me that five links to children have been made by their social workers: one for a sibling group and four for single children. That's all she could tell me. The details will have gone to Miranda, so if she thinks they are worth pursuing she'll let us know, I guess. We will ask her when she comes to visit in a couple of weeks.

The other thing she mentioned was the Adoption Register's exchange days, where social workers from local authorities and voluntary agencies attend with information about their approved adopters; some prospective adopters also turn up with copies of their own profiles. On the other side of the exchange are social workers who are family-finding for the children in their care. Everyone shares information in order to make a link that may lead to a match. I had thought that your local authority or agency had to invite you to come along to these events, but the woman I spoke to explained that once you are on the Register you don't need to go through your agency, so she's going to send us an invitation for the next exchange day, which takes place in December.

Friday 4th September
Miranda has finally sent us the first draft of our profile for family finders in other agencies. We think it's quite a nice profile, even if it has taken a while to get it sorted. We'll see how social workers react to it.

Monday 7th September
Jonathan and Stuart came over for lunch yesterday. We had a lovely afternoon catching up. Their son Connor is a real reminder of how things can turn out OK when it comes to adoption. After reading *Adoption Today* and all those books on adoption, sometimes you find yourself thinking that all placements are destined to end in disruption or with desperate parents who feel like they've failed their children. Yesterday Connor was perfectly behaved, ate everything, was playful, curious, and happy to chat to us and get us involved in his games...I was going to write that they've been really lucky with him but I know he's not been all sweetness and smiles since they adopted him and I'm sure a lot of how well he's settled has to do with how well they are bringing him up. No doubt we'll be asking them a million questions about how they did it in due course!

Wednesday 9th September
Uruguay today became the first Latin American country to allow gay civil partnerships and adoption by gay couples. It's great when countries in Latin America or Spain, which are seen as deeply Catholic, pass such laws. It helps break down barriers for others.

Monday 14th September
Elton John and David Furnish were all over the news today. They've announced they would like to adopt a fourteen-month-old Ukrainian boy they met at a centre for children of HIV-positive parents. The adoption may not be achievable as Ukraine does not allow gay adoptions and

they have a rule that parents cannot be older than the child by more than 45 years. Also, as the boy has a brother, they would need to adopt both children.

The way it's been reported, the story appears to be that although David Furnish had wanted to adopt for a while, Elton John has only been keen on the idea for the last couple of weeks. To go from nothing to openly talking about it in the press in the space of a fortnight seems like not a lot of thought has gone into the decision, and adopting is not something one does on impulse.

A *Daily Mail* columnist criticises Elton John's suitability. She bases her argument against the adoption on the fact that Elton is gay. Talking about the fourteen-month-old and his brother, she says that what they need is a mum and dad.

A writer in the *Daily Telegraph* objects to the adoption on the basis of the behaviour that Elton John displayed in the documentary, *Tantrums and Tiaras*, filmed in 1996. I hope nobody is ever going to judge my suitability to be a parent based on how I behaved 13 years ago! More worryingly, he states that, as an adopted gay man himself, he has no desire to have children of his own, and he thinks that it's in the best interests of the child to be with a man and woman. So now we have gay adopted reporters saying that a child's best interest is to be adopted by a heterosexual couple. I can't help but wonder what kind of research the writer has done before making such a statement. Is he just talking from his own experience? Since he was not adopted by a same-sex couple, how has he arrived at his conclusion? He ends his article by suggesting Elton John should adopt a cat instead. To say to someone who wants to adopt (regardless of who they are or how impulsive the decision is) that they should adopt a cat is insulting.

If that's really what they want I wish them luck and I hope they succeed. It would be great if there were several high-profile gay adopters for people to see that there's nothing wrong with gay adoption.

Thursday 17th September

I spent the whole morning unable to concentrate at work, wondering if Miranda would bring any news today. When she arrived, she showed us the profiles of two boys. She wanted to know if they were the sort of children we might go for. Both Mike and I read the profiles (they were two-page summaries, not full reports) and agreed that they sounded like a possible match. She said that they're more of a sample to get an idea, as these children have had quite a few links, but she had sent their social worker our profile, just in case. She also mentioned, in passing, another child of Mediterranean descent whose details have been sent to her. When we asked if there was anything more she could tell us about that child, she just said that it was 'bubbling away'.

Miranda wanted to know if any children in the magazines had caught our eye, and we mentioned a sibling group. We asked her whether the fact that they are featured in a magazine automatically means that there's something in their history that makes them hard to place. She said that might not be the case if the children are over five years of age or part of a sibling group. There aren't that many adopters willing to take "older" children or more than one child at a time, and so some authorities feature those children in magazines although they are not necessarily hard to place for other reasons.

We told Miranda about the adoption exchange days and she's happy for us to go to the one in December. I brought up the links that the woman at the Adoption Register had mentioned, and she said that she was following up some of those. We have agreed that she will only let us know of prospective links if it looks like they may get somewhere, so it's going to be difficult to know what's happening (if anything) behind the scenes. In any case, Miranda will get in touch in a couple of months for an update.

Finally, Miranda warned us that unless we've found a link within the next month (highly unlikely, considering she wasn't exactly optimistic or bombarding us with potential suggestions) then nothing will probably happen until the new year. They don't like to do introductions or have children move at around Christmas time, as it may be confusing or distressing for them. I know it's only three-and-a-half months, but still. We've only just got back from 'Nothing happens in the summer because social workers are on holiday' and we're now into 'Everything stops at Christmas'. No wonder so many children are waiting to be adopted!

Tuesday 22nd September
Although Mike has continued with a lot of the Beavers' activities during the summer, I haven't been to the nursery where I volunteer since July. On Monday I went back for the beginning of term to work with a new group. They were a bit shy when I first came into their classroom, but after a couple of hours they were trying to hug me and climb on me (you have to discourage physical contact so I had to put them down gently). The staff, all female, are referred to as Miss This, Mrs That, or as "auntie", so the kids don't really know what to call me. As one of the mums came to pick up her son, he pointed at me and said, 'We've got a new auntie!'

Wednesday 23rd September
Although the major work on the loft conversion finished a few weeks ago, we have just had the last of the new carpets put down. It finally feels like it's all done!

The problem we faced today was trying to work out what goes where now that we have a new room. The big decision was how many "spare" rooms to leave more or less empty. "How many rooms..." that sounds like we live in a mansion! We don't. We had a three-bedroom house and now with the loft conversion we have four. So one is our bedroom, another is the new room in the loft – which is now a guest bedroom but also serves as Mike's study when he works from home – and we have two others. One's my study and the other was the old guestroom. That room is now empty and we hope it will become the child's bedroom. But what to do about my study? We don't know whether to leave it empty as well. Miranda has told us that if we adopt two children and they've been used to sleeping in separate rooms, their social worker might prefer to keep that arrangement. I could work in the loft as well, but Mike and I trying to work in the same room is probably not a good idea. In the end we've decided to set up my study again. It's bad enough having one empty room. It feels a bit weird having a room that you don't use and that is emotionally charged with the possibility that it may one day be our child's bedroom – but also that it may not be.

And now that I think about it, it's a bit much to expect a family wanting to adopt two children to have a house with two "spare" rooms, isn't it? I grew up sharing a room with my brother and, although both of us would rather not have shared, that was the way it was and that was that. Mind you, if we were matched with a brother and sister it would make sense, I suppose.

Monday 28th September

It's been nearly two weeks since Miranda mentioned a sibling group and we can't seem to get them out of our heads. It's silly, but once you've read the details about a child, those details stay with you. Their names, ages, what they like to do...I suddenly find myself wondering how well they'd fit in with us (and we with them), if they'd like the house, if they'd get on with the kids we know who are of similar ages...It's just as well we're not being shown all the links Miranda's following or we'd go insane.

Monday 5th October

It was six months last Saturday since we went to the panel. Is six months too long to wait? No. At our preparation course we were told that the average wait in the UK from approval to matching is between nine months and a year. We were also warned to be prepared for a longer wait because we are a gay couple. We know of many couples who have waited a lot longer, but we also know of couples who had a child placed with them six months after the panel. It's impossible to tell how much of it comes down to us being a gay couple, the number of children we feel able to adopt, their ages, our local authority, our social worker, or just pure luck.

I think what's frustrating is that Miranda said that because we were willing to consider adopting more than one child, the wait was likely to be shorter. In fact, way back in April, she advised me not to book a work trip for October as by then she expected something to have happened. Because of that, we had October in our minds – and now we have to adjust and I've missed out on my trip for nothing.

Friday 9th October

Miranda emailed us a child's profile yesterday. It's for a boy just over a year old. He looks incredibly sweet in the picture. We read every word several times: he has a number of serious syndromes, both physical and mental, as well as some hereditary issues. In addition, there is uncertainty about his future development. We Googled some of the conditions to make sure we knew what they were (some conditions sound terrible with their complicated names and end up not being as serious as they seemed initially) and we didn't have to talk for long to decide that there are way too many issues for us to consider taking it any further.

We want to be parents, not carers.

This morning I replied to Miranda thanking her for sending the profile and explaining that we did not wish to be considered for this child. In fairness, she had said in her email that she wasn't sure if he had too many problems. Today I've been wondering: why did she send it to us if she thought that? Was it to test the waters and see whether we'd got to the stage when we're willing to take on a child that falls outside the limits we set? Is it to prove the infamous theory that gay men are so desperate that they'll take the children that nobody else wants? Or is it just her way of shutting us up? After all, we've been chasing her to send us profiles. It's probably just a profile that landed on her desk and she sent on just in case – and I'm "overthinking" about it.

Monday 12th October

Yesterday we went to an adopters' day out that our local authority organises every year at a nearby park. I had queried with Miranda whether we had been invited by mistake, as we have obviously not adopted yet, and she said that we should come as it would be good to meet other adopters and chat with them. We figured it would be a bit like going to the New Family Social get-togethers, so we agreed to go.

When we got there we were told that we and one single prospective adopter were the only people who hadn't adopted yet. The room was full of parents and kids. We sat at a table with two couples and their children. One of the couples was Rebecca and Alan. The other couple were very pleasant and have two gorgeous boys. It was really weird to have a conversation with someone you've literally just met about how long they waited, how it was going and so on, but it was nice to meet them.

Miranda came over to talk to us and we mentioned the profile she'd sent us last week. She hadn't been to the office and hadn't read our reply. It turns out she'd completely forgotten she'd sent it! After we reminded her, she agreed that the boy in question had too many issues but said that she'd sent it to us anyway because she 'wanted to be sure'. We asked about the sibling groups we'd discussed last time she came to visit us. She hasn't heard anything back about either group.

We also saw Miranda's supervisor, the one who did our second opinion interview. She asked us how the wait was going and then she said that she thought it was very unlikely that we'll be linked with a child from outside our local authority, which we understood as "who's going to want you other than us?".

Then Miranda introduced us to the prospective single adopter. She's been waiting for two years. We chatted about what it's like to wait, putting your life on hold, the frustration...in the end we were the last three people in the room, so the social workers came to tell us it was time to go. We jokingly said that we weren't going until they'd found us some children!

I was so annoyed and frustrated I could have cried. Not only were we made to go and sit with a whole load of people who have successfully adopted (Bridget Jones would no doubt make a reference to being a singleton in a room full of "smug marrieds" – absolutely nothing against the lovely people we talked to, but at the end of the day they've got what we're waiting for) but then also being introduced to someone who is, understandably, quite bitter about our local authority and how long she's had to wait. Add to that the comment from the supervisor about the likelihood of us adopting from elsewhere and it's just depressing.

Yesterday was also the day for the New Family Social get-together (which we obviously couldn't attend because we were at this adopters' day out). The contrast between both events couldn't be any greater. I think the biggest difference between them is that one is organised by adopters for other adopters and would-be adopters who *want* to be there and the other is organised by social workers for people who feel they *should* be there.

Incidentally, one thing that became clear through the different conversations we had with several people throughout the day is that nobody likes Miranda when they first meet her! Whenever we mentioned that she is our social worker people had a look on their faces that seemed to say "poor you"…so at least we know we weren't the only ones who found her hard to warm to at first.

Monday 19th October

Last Friday we decided that we need to be a lot more proactive if we want to be matched. I know we'd agreed to let our social worker and the local authority do their thing for a year before taking things into our own hands, but after last Sunday we fear that if we don't do anything about it, nothing may happen at all. The sibling group that we'd asked Miranda to enquire about appeared again in this month's magazine, which means that their social worker has probably looked at our profile and decided that it was worth featuring them for longer rather than getting more information about us.

So Mike and I had a chat and decided to pay for an online subscription to another of the child listing services. We had a look at their online profiles and immediately found two boys who looked like a good possibility, so I made an online enquiry about them. I emailed Miranda to let her know that we'd sent the enquiry and she replied to acknowledge my message and to say that she is talking to several authorities via the Adoption Register. We're a bit puzzled by this as last Sunday she intimated that there was nothing for us. Is this her way of letting us know that something is in the pipeline? Or just her reaction to our proactive approach: suddenly keen to show that she is doing her bit as well?

Friday 23rd October

Today, among the online profiles, I found the details of a boy who instantly seemed like a good match to me. The profile had a video clip, which made him much more real than any other profiles we've seen. I showed it to Mike and he could tell from the accent that he's currently living somewhere near where Mike's family come from. This made him feel a connection to the child. I tried to enquire about him online, but the facility to do so wasn't working, so I rang the office that runs the service and they gave me the boy's social worker's contact details. I rang her but got no reply, so I emailed our profile to her. I also emailed Miranda to let her know.

Tuesday 27th October

Today we enquired about another boy from a different online service. He's quite a good match from a cultural point of view, so we think we may be more appealing to his social worker. It's weird, because we feel a bit like we're betraying the boy we enquired about four days ago. We never even seem to hear back from their social workers though, so it doesn't make sense to enquire about just one child at a time. Miranda says that having another possible link on the horizon helps to cope with the disappointment when a link falls through.

Saturday 31st October

Tonight is Hallowe'en. It's not a day that's ever bothered me: we get a few chocolates for the neighbours' kids and that's pretty much it. I was just thinking this morning that maybe this time next year we'll be carving pumpkins, dressing up, getting together with the neighbours, going trick-or-treating...Maybe next year.

Tuesday 3rd November

I recently saw the profile of a child which says that prospective adopters 'must be familiar with north-east England culture'. Is the culture of someone living in the north-east of England really that different from that of someone living somewhere else in the country? Will a child from the north-east of England really feel like he doesn't belong if he is brought up in Devon, for example? Are the cultural differences between regions of the same country really that important? Is it really a hurdle that the child won't be able to overcome? I think it's too restrictive and it's limiting the number of potential adopters who could be offering that child a home. But what do I know?

Thursday 5th November

I rang the social worker who is family-finding for the boy we enquired about a couple of weeks ago (the one that Mike felt a connection to) again. I'd been trying to reach her for a couple of days with no luck, but this time I managed to find her. She gave me a lot of background on the boy and asked me a few questions about us. I told her we weren't put off by the boy's history and background, and she told me that they were interested in us! She will ask Miranda for our Prospective Adopter's Report, but he's going to be featured in one of the magazines and they'll wait to see what the response is before making any decisions. She has promised to keep me informed.

I also had an email from the social worker who looks after one of the other boys we'd followed up, the one whose cultural background we thought was close to ours. It turns out he may have an inherited mental condition as well as several cognitive problems and issues at school. I forwarded the email to Mike to ask him what he thought. We both agreed not to proceed and to concentrate on the other boy.

To round off the day, when I got home there was a letter

from the Adoption Register with the invitation to one of their exchange days.

It's quite hard not to count chickens before they're hatched, but we're trying to be quite rational about the fact that a social worker is interested in us. It's the first positive response we've had to our profile. We'll see whether they are still interested when they get our full report. Even if the possible link with this boy fails (fingers crossed it won't!), at least it's nice to know that people can be interested in you.

Monday 9th November
I spoke to Miranda on Friday. She hasn't heard from the social worker of the boy we've been discussing, but she will contact her to send our report. I told her they won't be shortlisting for a while as they want to see if there is any interest from the feature in one of the magazines. She doesn't think that he will attract many enquiries because of his age (he's almost six). She didn't talk about anything happening on her side, so we can probably assume that the potential links she was following are not going any further.

Tuesday 10th November
When I was at the nursery school yesterday, one of the girls hugged this little boy and I asked him, in a rather heterosexist way I must admit, if she was his girlfriend. He replied 'No, she's not my girlfriend. Billy is my boyfriend'. Billy is another boy in the class. They are all four years old. I had to really suppress a laugh. Then I started thinking: if a child of ours had said that, we'd wonder if they thought that same-sex relationships were the norm. Or if they'd said that in front of other adults or a social worker, we'd be worried that they might assume we were trying to "turn" the child gay. As it is, it's just one of those comments that kids make, nothing else. But I can just see me "overthinking" something like that for hours on end!

Thursday 12th November

Yesterday Miranda rang to say that she'd spoken to the social worker of the boy we're interested in and they have agreed to exchange full profiles. They seem to have had a good discussion. Miranda said that she hadn't heard at all from the social workers of any of the other children we've enquired about and advised us to forget about them, as it has been quite a while. So we're only in the running for this child. It's quite annoying to see that some of those other children are still being featured in the magazines. It means that the reason they haven't got back to us is not that the children have been placed, but that they are still family finding for them and we're not being considered. It would be nice to at least get some feedback indicating why they don't want us, but I guess that's too much to ask for.

Miranda then mentioned that there is a child from our local authority that she couldn't say anything about there and then, but she wants to see us next week and we've arranged a visit. She's being very cagey and we have no idea what this is about. We can't help wondering if taking the other boy seriously, or being taken seriously by his social worker, has suddenly made her spring into action. After all, she did say that our local authority wanted to keep us for their own children. Whatever the reason, we're quite intrigued and looking forward to her visit next week!

Saturday 14th November

Today we watched an episode of the new US sitcom *Modern Family*. The show is a mockumentary about three families who are all related, including Mitchell and Cameron, a gay couple who have just adopted a little girl. Although they are to a certain extent stereotypical, as is every member of the other families, the actors, writers and directors clearly care about these characters. The gay adoption issue is actually a non-issue in the storyline, and it's for that reason that I think the programme should be applauded. Without being political or preachy, it gives visibility and a sense of normality to gay adoption. And it's very funny.

Monday 16th November

The *Telegraph* ran an article on Sunday to coincide with National Adoption Week. According to a senior member of the Government's parenting academy, children brought up by lesbians are no more likely to be gay than those brought up by heterosexual parents.

We're looking forward to tomorrow's visit. We're very intrigued by whatever news Miranda's bringing!

Tuesday 17th November

Miranda came to see us today. She gave us a copy of the Child Permanence Report (CPR) for the boy we've been enquiring about. Then she told us about the mysterious child she wouldn't talk about on the phone. He has a horrific family history. In fact, she didn't really talk about the child; she just described his background to see whether we think we could cope with it, and only if we think we can, will she give us more details about him. All she would say about him was that he is a boy and he's under two.

After she left, Mike and I were a bit numb trying to process this information. We will need more time to make a decision.

In the meantime, we've read the CPR for the other boy, which is not happy reading but at least doesn't come with any shocking surprises. After my conversation with his family finder it was pretty much what we were expecting. This is the first full CPR we have seen, so it's a bit of a milestone. Miranda said his family finder was interested in us and that she'd liked the things I asked and said when we spoke on the phone. It was very strange trying to concentrate on this boy and the progress we're making with him, and at the same time still have the information about the other boy in our heads, so we may have to read it again after we've made a decision about the boy with the horrific history. That boy's circumstances are more extreme than we ever thought we would need to consider or have ever read about in any of the books, magazines or websites.

Thursday 19th November
We received an email from Miranda: the social worker for the boy whose CPR we received on Wednesday wants to visit us! We're very excited but trying to keep calm. At the very least it's one step closer. Miranda hasn't mentioned dates at all. She noticed that his CPR was over a year old and has requested an update as a lot may have changed since it was written.

We have been thinking a lot about the boy with the horrific history. I wrote to Miranda to ask her about the after-adoption support available should he be placed with us.

It's somewhat hard to balance the positive news while dealing with this other child. To add to the mix, we have asked Miranda to enquire about another child that appeared in one of the magazines. We are very keen on the one we've made progress with, but she has stressed to us that we shouldn't put all our eggs in one basket and to keep looking.

Just to recap on our enquiries so far:

- Boys A and B (siblings): Miranda found them for us but never heard back from their social worker after she enquired.
- Boys C and D (siblings): we saw them in a magazine and asked Miranda to follow up on our behalf. She never heard back from their social worker.
- Boy E: Miranda sent us his profile but we felt he had too many health and mental problems for us to cope with.

- Boys F and G (siblings): we found their profile online and made an enquiry but never heard back.
- Boy H: we found his profile online and made contact with the social worker directly. We both felt a connection to him straight away, especially Mike. He is the one whose social worker wants to visit us.
- Boy I: we found his profile online and made an enquiry directly. We thought he was a good ethnic match. His social worker sent us a fuller profile and we felt that there were too many health and mental uncertainties.
- Boy J: Miranda has asked us to consider his horrific family history before giving us any further details. We are still trying to find out more before making a decision.
- Boy K: We found him in one of the magazines. Have just asked Miranda to enquire on our behalf.

To be honest we're only enquiring about boy K because we feel that we mustn't get carried away and we don't want to be left without options or anything to look forward to if H turns out not to be the one for us.

Monday 23rd November
We spent last Saturday with friends we hadn't seen in a while. Their children, seven and four, were great with us and although they normally ask me to play with them, this time they were keener on playing with Mike. I was really pleased about this as Mike always worries that he's no good with children. On Sunday we caught up with Jonathan and Stuart. We chatted a bit about the latest developments and they agreed that the decision we have taken regarding Boy J (with the horrific background) is the right one.

It took us five days of thinking long and hard about it, but we have decided not to express an interest in this boy. We really feel that we'd be forever worried about how to reply to questions, and how he would feel later in life about his identity and family history. We don't feel we're qualified or experienced enough to give the kind of support this boy will need, as much as we would love to. We haven't taken this decision lightly; it's been a very hard choice to make. Now we want to put the whole thing behind us and focus on H.

Thursday 26th November

I spoke to Miranda yesterday. She said she understood why we had turned down Boy J. We received the update on H this morning and we're still very keen to proceed. Miranda is busy for the rest of the week and she told me to get in touch next Tuesday to let her know if we want to proceed with a visit from his social workers. She wasn't sure if the visit will take place before or after Christmas, as it will depend on everyone's schedules. I know Christmas is only a month away, but now that we're geared up and things seem to be progressing, we just want to get on with it! Still, we're very happy with the way things are going so we'll just have to be patient for a bit longer.

Tuesday 1st December

Our friends Gavin and Sue have received good news at last. It looks like the children who were "withdrawn" while the judge decided whether the birth family deserved another chance will have placement orders after all. It may sound bad to say that we're pleased that the siblings won't be reunited with their birth family, but there are very good reasons for it and Gavin and Sue can offer them a wonderful home. I really hope it works out for them.

Mike spoke to Miranda today to confirm that we want to go ahead with a visit from H's social workers. Apparently his family finder is on holiday this week and Miranda is on holiday the week after next, so either it happens next week or it will most likely happen after Christmas.

Tomorrow we're going to the Adoption Register exchange day. I'm really not looking forward to it for a number of reasons. For starters we're very keen on the link with H and we don't really want to look for other children. Another reason is that I keep expecting this exchange day to be like a used car forecourt. "Take this child and get a free sibling!", "Damaged children clearance!" Seriously, the thought of going from stall to stall looking at children's profiles as if they were goods for sale (and then having to sell ourselves as a potential match) is not exactly appealing.

Wednesday 2nd December
We turned up at the venue for the exchange day with plenty of time. We registered, had a quick briefing about what to expect, and went in to find a large room with 40 or so stalls displaying children's and adopters' profiles. The impression was that of a trade fair, which seemed horribly wrong but utterly practical. We approached the first stall unsure of what we were expected to do, but we soon got into it as we had more or less the same conversation at each stall. It went like this:

- Hi, what are you approved for?
- One or two children, nought to seven.
- Have you got a preference for boys or girls?
- Not really, although we have been told that we're more likely to be approved for boys.
- OK, let's see what we have here...

At this point they would look at their profiles and pull out the ones that matched our ethnicities and the details we had just given. Then they would talk to us about them and we'd pick up copies of profiles that we felt might be a good match.

A few of the agencies asked for our profile and we gave it to them. We left with the details of nine children including sibling groups. Of these, once we looked at them again, we have rejected three. The other six we're going to keep until we have heard about the visit from the social workers for H.

It was a very overwhelming and emotionally draining day. I really don't think I'd like to go back to another event like that.

On the positive side, no one seemed to bat an eyelid about us being a gay couple. We spotted at least one other male and one female couple. And no one mentioned it being a problem except a couple of profiles that specifically referred to looking for a male/female couple. I wasn't in the mood to challenge their social workers and ask them exactly why that was, although now I feel I should have.

Wednesday 9th December
I emailed Miranda last Sunday to ask if there was any news from H's family finder. It's been nearly three weeks since they said they would like to visit us and nothing's been arranged. Miranda tried to get in touch and finally managed to speak to them today. She called Mike this afternoon and told him that they are not sure now if they will be visiting us after all. Apparently there is another couple who have expressed an interest and they're keen to visit them too. They have also decided that they are going to feature him again in the magazine and on the website where we found him, so clearly they don't have high hopes that we're the right family for him. Apparently, after they got our full Prospective Adopter's Report, they were concerned about Mike's relationship with his dad and brother.

The social workers have now confirmed that they will not be visiting this side of Christmas. Miranda has suggested some dates at the beginning of January and they will be letting her know at the end of the week whether they want to come at all. Mike says that Miranda's tone implied that she thought this was a gentle way to let us down and by the end of the week it will be a "no", but I've not given up hope. We will be very disappointed if it's a "no", but we don't know for sure and this may end up being just a few weeks' delay. Mike is quite down, as he feels that it's because of his family that they're no longer so keen on us, but clearly it's not his fault at all.

Friday 11th December
Yesterday we were both so down about H that we emailed his family finder directly and asked her to consider visiting us so they can judge our suitability on the basis of meeting us face-to-face rather than just on our report. We had no reply, so we assume that it isn't good news.

Today I emailed Miranda to let her know I'd written to the family finder, since I'd forgotten to copy her into the email yesterday. She was supposed to get back to us today with news about whether H's social worker and family finder have decided to visit us or not. By 3.30 she hadn't, so once again we assumed the worst. Then I had an email from the family finder: we are still in the running! She said that there must have been some sort of misunderstanding because they'd told Miranda that there were many strong points in our report. They are visiting the other couple, but they will come and visit us as well. No date yet, but we're over the moon. It looks like a "no" has turned into a "maybe". And at the very least we'll be able to meet them and present ourselves directly and not through a report that we didn't write.

The family finder's email mentioned that Miranda had said we had been looking at another boy's CPR – which is not true – and this is why they'd put us aside. This may have been either yet another misunderstanding, or Miranda has been misleading them. Why she would want to, I don't know.

Miranda actually rang later and was clearly angry with

us for having been in contact directly with the family finder. She said we appeared desperate and needed to be patient as we're still a long way away from being matched. She insisted that all she'd said to them was that we had been looking at another child (Boy J). We have no reason to believe one social worker over the other, so for now we'll go with the explanation that it's all been a misunderstanding.

I managed to pacify Miranda and she agreed to call the family finder and try to get dates. She never called us back so we'll have to wait ten days, when she's back from her own annual leave, to hear of possible dates for the visit.

Although we've been all over the place today, the final outcome is that we started this morning fearing that we wouldn't get a visit after all and we're finishing it knowing that they do want to visit us. That's good enough for the next ten days while we wait for further news.

Monday 14th December
We went to the New Family Social Christmas get-together yesterday and had a great time. There were around 40 adopters (with their children) and prospective adopters. We caught up with quite a few people we hadn't seen in a while, some we had seen not that long ago, and met some new prospective adopters. It's funny that the first time we went we were completely new to it, and now we meet other people who are new, and we can share some of our experience with them.

Tuesday 15th December
Rebecca and Alan have been granted the adoption order for their daughter. This means that she is now theirs forever and they needn't have any further involvement from the social workers. They are very happy and we are happy for them. We've been invited to their adoption day celebration, and are looking forward to it.

Who knows? Maybe one day that will be us too. I know

I long not only for the day we have a child or children, but also for the day we don't have to deal with social workers any more!

It's quite amazing that Rebecca and Alan started the process at the same time as we did and have now finished it. Gavin and Sue started at least a year before them and they're still waiting. It proves that each case is individual and there's no specific timeframe.

Sunday 20th December
On Thursday the Portuguese Government approved their gay marriage bill. It has yet to be passed by parliament, but it should get through in January and the law would then come into effect in April. As usual, the church and the conservatives are up in arms and demanding a referendum.

The law, however, forbids gay adoption. Local gay rights organisations have complained as the previous law didn't make a reference to sexual orientation, thus making it possible for single gay people to adopt without declaring their sexuality. So it looks like Portugal is taking one step forward and one backwards in gay rights.

Monday 21st December
We had a message from Miranda. She's been trying to get hold of the family finder for H but had no luck. She says she'll call us tomorrow so hopefully she may have some news then.

Thursday 24th December
We haven't heard from Miranda at all, so we're not expecting to receive any news regarding an interview until January now.

Despite the weather and flight cancellations everywhere I managed to get to Spain last Tuesday, so I've spent the last couple of days surrounded by excited children. The kids and I put the decorations up today along with the tree and the nativity and so far everything's still standing and in place.

Friday 25th December

Two years ago I hoped that by last Christmas we'd have been approved and maybe matched (we weren't). Last year I assumed we'd have been approved in February (in the end it took another two months) and hopefully matched by the end of the year (we haven't). This year is different because we're not wondering about an abstract child: we're hoping to be matched with H and I can't help myself from wondering what he's doing today and hoping that next year he'll be with us. It's not healthy, I know. But if you can't hope at Christmas, when can you?

Wednesday 30th December

I am back in the UK now after a week in Spain. Miranda rang this afternoon to say that H's social worker and family finder are definitely coming to visit us in two weeks' time. Apparently they have another update and a report from his school for us. Miranda's asked us to look up information about local schools and post-adoption support in our local area.

Miranda said that the social workers sounded positive, and we're very happy with the news, but desperately trying not to get too excited. We know they're visiting another couple, so it's a competitive "match". Still, it's excellent news and a very promising end to the year.

5

2010

Friday 1st January

Yesterday we told a few friends and family about the fact that we're expecting a visit. Today I regretted it, because if we're not successful we'll have to tell them about that as well. It's a very difficult balance to strike between not getting carried away and not feeling like you're hiding things from the people you're close to.

Sunday 3rd January

Since we've had the visit confirmed it's been hard to get it off our minds. Mike and I will be talking about something completely different, or watching TV or whatever and then one of us will suddenly say: 'What will we ask?', 'Shall we volunteer information about this or that?' and stuff like that. I don't think I'll be able to concentrate much at work for the next two weeks...

Talking of volunteering information, one piece of information I wanted to mention to the social workers is that we're monogamous. I know that some people think of gay men as promiscuous even if they are in a long-term relationship, and I want to let them know that we're not. I have nothing against people who are in open relationships or whatever (each to their own), but we aren't. Mike thinks that if we say that, it may come across like we're protesting too much because we *are* promiscuous. He may have a point. We'll ask Miranda what she thinks. I just don't want to be judged due to some prejudice and not address it. But if I address it, I may be opening a can of worms. Do heterosexual couples worry about this?

Wednesday 6th January

We spent a couple of hours yesterday re-reading H's Child Permanence Report again and came up with a whole list of clarifications and updates that we'd like to have when the social workers come to see us next week. We also tried to come up with answers to the questions that we think they will ask us, including more stuff about Mike's family, why we've chosen H, and the difficult question of the last name. Mike and I kept our names when we got married, and Miranda says we need to decide which last name the boy would have. We've been playing with possible combinations, but, perhaps unsurprisingly, we each like our own last name best...

I also looked at the website where we first saw H and noticed that he's not featured any more. He didn't appear in the latest print issue either. Does this mean that they're positive about finding a match for him? In that case, if the information we've received about them interviewing just one other couple is correct, we have a 50/50 chance! Mike is preparing for bad news, but the way I'm choosing to see this is that at least we've got as far as a visit. Let's see how much further we can make it.

Thursday 7th January

Miranda came today to help us get ready for next week's visit. We spent the morning going through the questions that we had prepared, some of which she didn't think were appropriate, and discussing what we could expect to be asked and how best to answer. She also suggested getting rid of the knife block in the kitchen (in case it's seen as a potential danger) and rearranging the sofas in the living room. We thought she might be quite cautious, as she always is, but she genuinely seems to believe we have an equal chance with the other couple they'll be seeing, so that's as good as we can hope for, I guess. We have no idea when they'll be visiting the other couple, so we don't know when we'll be likely to get an answer after our visit.

Monday 11th January
We've been busy preparing for tomorrow's visit. We've caught up with our notes on the Permanence Report and other documentation, brushed up on all the adoption key words, cleaned the house, rearranged the furniture and hidden our knife block. If someone had told me at the beginning of this process that moving our sofas would help us adopt a child, I'd have questioned it. We've now got to the stage where we don't question things any more and just get on with it. Whatever the social workers suggest, we do. Move the furniture? Of course!

We can't think what else needs doing. All we can hope for is to do our best to be ourselves and answer all their questions. Fingers crossed!

Tuesday 12th January
The first thing I thought about this morning when I woke up was that today our lives could change forever. It's a weird feeling and a difficult one to manage. We spent the morning reading the reports and going over our questions once again and we managed to get to lunchtime without getting too nervous. At 1.30 Miranda arrived and we chatted until H's family finder and social worker arrived at 2, as planned. They gave us an update on H and how he's progressed since the last report. They then announced that

they're no longer considering the other family – good! But that he will definitely feature in one of the family-finding magazines next month – not so good. We asked the questions we had prepared and they showed us some more recent pictures. It was very special to see how he's grown since the pictures we'd seen so far were taken, but we weren't allowed to keep them. They then asked us to clarify some points in our PAR and explained what happens next. They had a quick look at the house, which they seemed to like. Sarah, H's social worker, asked if the house is always this tidy and I had to admit to a bit of over-cleaning! They left shortly after and promised to be in touch soon. Miranda stayed behind. She felt the meeting had gone really well. She asked us whether we wanted some time to give her our answer, but we were both very happy for her to let them know that yes, we are still interested.

The social workers have agreed they will get in touch with Miranda on Thursday to ask her whether we still want to go ahead and let her know whether they want to go any further. If they do, then they will arrange a second visit, with H's foster carer. If that goes well then they hope to get things going as quickly as possible.

This is a lot to get our heads around. On the one hand it's very encouraging; on the other hand, there are a lot of "ifs" involved. So we're left in a bit of a limbo, not knowing whether to be excited or not. In any case, we are very pleased with the way the visit went. Roll on Thursday!

Thursday 14th January

Miranda rang this morning to let us know that H's social worker and family finder have been in touch and, yes, they want to go ahead with us! Apparently they were very pleased that we'd also said yes. They've arranged another visit in a couple of weeks. This time it will be just Sarah, his social worker, and Annie, his foster carer. Annie should be able to give us lots of first-hand information about H and answer our questions (we have so many!). Apparently they really trust her opinion, so the decision is likely to be largely based on what she thinks of us.

We are so happy. We are trying to keep our feet on the ground, though. We realise this could still go wrong, the foster carer may not like us, or the matching panel may go against us, but right now it feels right and we're allowing ourselves to believe that we may be daddies soon.

Friday 15th January

Yesterday we kept going from 'Let's keep calm' to 'We're going to be daddies!' and back. Today we're more 'Oh My God! Are these people insane? They are going to trust us with that boy? What if we're terrible?' I guess it's the nerves of accepting that what was always a hope and a dream may actually turn into reality. We think that we are as prepared as one can be in these situations and we firmly believe that we can provide a good home for H, help him recover from the past trauma in his life, and create a family.

We're being quite good at not going to the shops and buying every piece of furniture his room will need or going into every local school to request a place for him. Miranda told us there'll be time for that if it gets to that stage. We have done some research online for schools, and I suppose we could have a look at beds etc. just to get an idea of models and prices...

Tuesday 19th January

Since we first saw his profile, H has turned six. This is older than I originally pictured when thinking about adoption. Our preparation course and the books we've read on attachment have dispelled the myth that a younger child is less traumatised by their loss of the birth family, and speaking to our social worker and looking at the family finding magazines, it anyway soon became obvious that there aren't that many children under two who are free for adoption. Considering that gay couples tend not to be exactly at the top of the wishlist for family finders, our chances of a younger child are even smaller. Older children, like H, are probably aware of why they had to be adopted. Many of them remember the abuse or neglect they suffered, and that does mean that it's easier for them to understand why they cannot live with their birth parents. They can also understand that they are safer in their new environment.

As for learning Spanish...well, I've had to compromise on that one. I hope that meeting his Spanish cousins, aunt, uncle and grandparents will encourage an older child to want to learn the language.

Monday 25th January

We decided to book ourselves on a last-minute break and spent the last five days freezing our pants off in Denmark. We managed to switch off from work, jobs around the house that still need doing, paperwork...it was great. We had a chance to be just us, by ourselves, and also to talk. We both really hope the match with H goes ahead. We're as sure as we can be about a child that we've never met!

Tuesday 26th January

For the last couple of months H hasn't been featured on the website where we originally found him, but yesterday I checked online and he's there again. We knew this would happen, but it still was really hard to see him "advertised". I hadn't realised just how "attached" we've got to him already. I just really wanted the website to crash, or the magazine to have some sort of printing error when it comes out in the next few days. I don't want anyone else to see him and enquire about him. What if a "perfect couple" express an interest? Would his social workers consider them and make us wait until they've made a decision? Maybe drop us for someone else? It's not a nice feeling.

Wednesday 27th January

We've been preparing questions for tomorrow's visit. Originally we had pages and pages, adapted from questions people have posted on the Adoption UK messageboard and from questions that other prospective adopters have suggested. In the end we've decided to leave most of them for introductions, if we get to that stage, when there should be plenty of time to chat and find some of the answers for ourselves.

So tomorrow we're planning to ask about:

- His weekday routine
- His weekend routine
- Things he likes to do: Play games? Watch TV? Read books? Cooking? Crafts? Favourite toys?
- Sleeping habits: wake up time? Naps? Bedtime?
- Food: allergies, favourite food, disliked foods, portions, mealtimes…
- Likes and dislikes: e.g. music and noise, animals, clothing, outdoor or indoor play
- School: academic and behavioural issues
- Speech and understanding
- Relationships with other children (in foster home/school)
- Any photos/mementos/memory box or book the foster carers might have made so far
- Any special trips with birth family or foster carers?
- Any particular triggers for memories of siblings, parents, "old life"?
- General health: colds, digestion. Any operations? Any hereditary conditions?
- What has he been told about us? Has someone talked to him about the possibility of having two dads? Has he had books such as *And Tango Makes Three?*

I expect we'll come up with new ones as we go along and we'll skip some others. We're mostly looking forward to hearing lots about him directly from Annie, the foster carer, who's known him for quite a while now, although of course we realise we're going to be asked questions as well.

Thursday 28th January

We were dreading that the foster carer would hate us or that she wouldn't be so keen on H going to live with a gay couple, and worried that this would influence the local authority's decision or impact on the introductions period. But all our fears were unfounded. I'm not sure what I expected her to be like, but she was very warm, very friendly, and very funny! She had us laughing within five minutes of walking through the door. She was very professional too. We talked about H, and she answered all our questions. She also gave us some pictures that she had taken this morning. The social workers frowned at this, and said that we'd need to return them if the match doesn't go ahead. Everything she said about H and how far he's come since he went into foster care was encouraging. She gave us good advice about what to expect and how to deal with his behaviour. She clearly wanted to make sure that H will be well looked after and that we're prepared for the challenges ahead. She also conveyed to us how much she clearly thinks of him and how much she wants him to move on to a good permanent family. We were reassured that H has been in a good home whilst in care (and a little intimidated to have to live up to her standards), and that introductions will be made easier by her and her husband, whom we've yet to meet, but who sounds just as nice.

We were on our own with Annie for a few minutes while we showed her around the house, and she took the opportunity to give us her phone number in case we come up with any other questions. She also told us that she thinks we will make good parents for him. We were moved by her encouragement.

H's social workers will get in touch with Miranda soon – hopefully by tomorrow – to let us know how they want to proceed. Before they left, I mentioned that H has appeared in the magazine again, and they reassured us that any enquiries they get will be shelved and everyone will be told that the child has been linked.

Once they had gone, Miranda told us that she thought the visit had gone well and gave us provisional dates that they've pencilled in for the planning meeting, matching panel, and introductions. We are beginning to believe this may be it, but we'll wait until tomorrow before we celebrate.

Friday 29th January

We didn't hear from Miranda all morning, so we almost convinced ourselves that they'd decided against us after all. At 2.15 she finally heard from the family finder and called us straight away: we have made a very good impression on the foster carer and the social workers and all is going ahead. We were very relieved and we had a little cry after we put the phone down.

The next steps are for H's social worker to write a placement plan and an adoption support plan, which Miranda will then complete and we will be asked to comment on. After that there will be a planning meeting mid-February, when all the social workers, the foster carers and we will get together and plan the introductions. If all goes according to plan, we could go to the panel in early March and hopefully begin introductions after Easter!

We are over the moon. I can't find words to describe the feeling – always a little tempered by the fact that we still have the last hurdle of the matching panel looming. All the months of decisions, preparation, approval, and waiting seem completely worth it to get to where we are. We are ecstatic, and we can't wait for all these things to happen so we can meet him soon. We've had phone calls and texts from lots of friends and family all afternoon and are quite overwhelmed by their support and how happy everyone is for us.

Wednesday 3rd February
It's five weeks until we go to the matching panel and I really wish it were tomorrow. Now that we know much more about H and we've met his foster carer, we just can't wait. We're finding it very hard to concentrate at work, and I'm also struggling with the fact that I haven't told most of my colleagues. Today we had a meeting in the office to plan our activities for the latter part of this year and I felt bad talking about my contribution when, if all goes well, I will actually be on adoption leave, but I can't say anything yet.

We've been holding back so far and have never bought anything for a possible son as we didn't want to take anything for granted, but today we actually spent several hundred pounds on furniture to go into H's room. I know we really should have waited until the panel, but there is normally a few weeks' wait for furniture delivery, and we won't have many weeks from the panel to needing to take a picture of the bedroom for the introduction book, so we thought "what the hell" and just went ahead and ordered it all. It really is madness to buy furniture just so that you can take a picture of it, and of course, if things go wrong, we'll have this furnished room that will feel quite eerie and only remind us of what might have been. But we're going with the thought that the panel will say "yes". We can't do everything at the last minute! That's our excuse anyway.

Tuesday 9th February
Miranda rang yesterday to ask us for dates to visit H's current school. We're going to his local authority next week for the planning meeting and we had hoped to talk to his teachers on the same day, but it's half-term so we'll need to

go back another time. We can't do anything about looking for a school in our area until after the planning meeting, when we'll have a better idea of both when he might come to live with us and how long they want him to stay off school while he settles with us.

Adoption UK are running a course on attachment next month and we asked Miranda if this was something that might be worth attending, but she doesn't think there is much point in going for two reasons: she thinks we've done our homework with all the reading on attachment and adoption and that we are very "in tune" with H. Apparently this is what his social workers and foster carer said. Also, we're getting special training from his local authority. This is called attachment-focused counselling and will require a few sessions, of which two should take place after the panel but before placement. We're really pleased about this as obviously we welcome any opportunity for training, and also because it shows that the local authority is being proactive in supporting its adopters. We're getting absolutely no allowance from them other than our travel expenses during introductions. Some people may get grants, or a settling in allowance, but apparently this particular authority does not provide that. It would have been nice to get something to help with the costs, but at the end of the day we should get used to the expense of having a child!

We spoke to Miranda again today and she confirmed that she's received the placement and adoption support plans from H's social worker. She now has to fill in her bit and then she will send it to us so we can digest it before the planning meeting. H's family finder also got in touch today to let us know that she's sent us the psychological reports on the birth parents completed during the care proceedings, which we're fairly sure will be hard to read, but with which we need to familiarise ourselves. The reports have been edited so that we can only see the parts that refer to H, and therefore preserve the privacy of his siblings, who have already been adopted. She also sent us some paperwork we need to complete.

It feels like things are on a roll. We're actually enjoying this part of the process, which we never thought we would. We are now even referring to 'when H is here'. Last Sunday some friends came over for lunch with their adopted son. I could really picture us getting together with theirs and ours in the not too distant future. Less than a month until the panel now!

Tuesday 15th February
On Saturday night we saw another gay couple we met through New Family Social and they've also been given a matching panel date for the end of the month – so it's good news all around. In fact they've been linked with a sibling group we enquired about (Boy F and Boy G). You don't normally find out what happens to these children, so it's really nice to know that those boys will be going to a good home.

We read the draft of the placement and support plans, which we commented on and fed back on today so they can be taken to the planning meeting on Thursday. And finally we wrote the first draft of the document we've been asked to provide for the panel with our views on the placement plan and why we would make good parents for H. We listed what we think are our strengths and how we would support him. We hope that's what they are looking for!

We also spent yesterday reading the psychological reports on H and his birth parents and they really weren't an easy read. Even though we know that the birth parents treated him badly, once you read about their own childhoods and personal circumstances, you can't help but feel sorry for them and understand, to a certain extent, the inevitability of why they did what they did.

The birth family obviously was in the back of my mind

when I went to sleep. I actually had a nightmare that woke me up at four this morning. In my nightmare the birth family had been told about us (we know that the local authority is going to tell them that a gay couple will be adopting their son), and they sold their story to the *Daily Mail*, which ran an article about us on their front cover! How's that for a truly terrifying thought? After everything that happened last year to the gay couple in Scotland, I guess it's a possibility that we'll have to live with until we know how the birth family has reacted. A remote possibility I hope!

Wednesday 17th February

My nightmare turned out to be a premonition! We received a phone call from Miranda earlier today explaining that H's birth parents have been informed of the plan to place their son with a gay couple and are "not keen" (her words). They are refusing to meet us and say that they will engage a solicitor to stop the placement. Miranda explained to us that the birth parents can oppose the placement order, but they cannot base their objections on the fact that we are gay, as that would be discriminatory. They would need to prove that it's in the child's best interest not to be placed for adoption at all or that their own circumstances have changed. From what we hear, they haven't.

We realise this may come to nothing, as they may not actually carry out their threat to go to a solicitor, and it may have been no more than a gut reaction on hearing about us. Even if they do go to a solicitor, they may get legal advice not to proceed. But nevertheless we are quite anxious about it. This is quite difficult to cope with because we do understand the instinct of wanting to keep your child and wanting the best for him. They obviously don't perceive gay parents as a good thing and we only wish we could meet them to assuage whatever doubts or negative preconceptions they may have.

Thursday 18th February

Today we had our planning meeting. As well as Miranda and us, also present were a chairperson, Sarah – H's social worker, his family finder, Annie – his foster carer, and her support worker. Annie brought more photos, which we were allowed to keep. We planned all of the introductions. We will meet H just after Easter and gradually spend more and more time with him. At the weekend the foster carers will bring him to our house and he'll spend at least one night here before he eventually moves in the following weekend. There will be two review meetings during introductions. H will have a say, and if he's reacting badly, his wishes and feelings will be taken into account, which we're glad to hear. The last thing we would want is to take home a child who doesn't want to live with us!

We had more information about the birth family and their reaction. Apparently, H's birth mother said 'he can't live with two men' and his birth father was the one who said he would go to a solicitor. The family finder thinks that the mother won't do anything about it but his father may. The most likely thing is that they won't get leave of court to challenge the placement order. However, all this could delay the placement, which is the last thing we want.

From what we understand, in most local authorities you go to the matching panel first and then, only after the match has been approved, do you have the planning meeting. But here it's the other way round, and making all these plans and decisions was a bit surreal knowing that we haven't been formally matched yet. Having got this far, it will be incredibly difficult and even harder to accept if the matching panel say "no". We just have to believe that it will happen.

Tuesday 23rd February

Yesterday I went to the nursery for the last time. I must admit that I signed up for it because we knew it would look good and the social workers had suggested we do it, but after nearly two years, I feel that it's been great training. I'm much more confident with kids and have really enjoyed it. They made a very sweet farewell card for me with their pictures and they all wrote their names on it. I was quite moved when they gave it to me and quite sad to say goodbye. I shall miss them. At least until H moves in, after which I expect I won't have the time!

Thursday 25th February
Miranda has got in touch: H's social worker has spoken to his parents again. They still are not keen on meeting us but the good news is that they haven't gone to a solicitor (yet). We think, and the social workers agree, that if they were thinking of going to a solicitor it would probably have been in the heat of the moment straight after being told. It may seem insensitive to hope the birth parents don't "interfere" with the process, but the thing is that they are not trying to stop H from being adopted, which I would understand; they are against him being adopted by a gay couple, and that doesn't exactly endear them to us.

In the meantime it's two weeks to the panel! We have now been sent the final placement plan with the full introductions schedule, the support plan, and the minutes of the planning meeting.

We have managed to produce a first draft of the book to introduce ourselves to H and we are planning a DVD, although we're not really sure what to film. We're hoping the weather improves so we can take pictures and film in brighter conditions, otherwise H will think we live in complete gloom! I've also started watching *Ben 10* (H's favourite cartoon series) to familiarise myself with the plot and characters...

Friday 26th February
We visited a possible school for H today. We have shortlisted

four schools and this one was at the bottom of our list as it's the one that's furthest away from the house; we would need to drive him, and the children he'd meet wouldn't be local to our area. On the plus side we know it's a good school academically, but we have also to consider their experience of looked-after children and the support they can provide. We thought that since it was our least favourite "on paper", it would be a good idea to visit it first to get some experience of meeting Heads and asking questions. To our surprise, we absolutely loved the school. It's not too big and there was a really good atmosphere. We went into every classroom and the children seemed to be engaged and not bored. The staff were brilliant too. When we spoke to the headteacher she seemed to be frank, thorough and interested in H. To top it all, his teacher would be a woman who has two adopted children, so she's very aware of the challenges. We are absolutely delighted, but of course we have another three schools to visit, so we won't make our minds up until we have. The decision about which school he will go to has to be made with his local authority and social workers, so their opinion will matter as well.

Thursday 4th March

On Tuesday we went to see a second school and today we visited our third. The second school was our favourite when we made our shortlist. It's very similar to the one that H attends at the moment. It has good rating scores and a good reputation. It's also a short drive from our house. When we got there the headteacher looked really stressed. We thought there must have been some sort of emergency going on, but then it dawned on us that it's her permanent state. She whizzed us around the school, talking more about their plans for the building than about what they do. As we walked around, the atmosphere felt quite chaotic. At one point, whilst talking to us, the headteacher started telling a child off, who just ignored her and walked on as she spoke. We weren't introduced to any of the teachers, and she made a point of telling us that the school was full. When we asked how the school would support H in case there were any issues with him having two dads, she replied that some of the parents in the school hold "certain views" and it would probably be best not to advertise it. She even suggested that only one of us turn up for parents' evenings! We smiled, thanked her for her time, walked out, and agreed that would be the last school we would ever want to send our son to. The whole thing was awful, and we didn't know whether she was just trying to put us off. She never asked us a single question about H: not the type of school he's currently at, nor how he's progressing there, not even his name! She just kept referring to him as "the child".

The third school we visited today was a much larger school with over 400 students. It's a ten-minute walk from our house, which is a big plus! We met the deputy Head, who was very nice and showed us the facilities and the classrooms. The children seemed well behaved and the atmosphere was pleasant. They currently have a looked-after child in the school and one of the boys has two mums. There have been some confrontations, but these were in response to this child being aggressive, and he's never been bullied because he has lesbian parents. The deputy Head was happy for the social workers to get in touch if necessary and seemed to have a good idea of the kind of support they could offer H. We felt the school was certainly an option, but nowhere near as suitable as the first school we visited last week.

Miranda rang to let us know that the panel medical adviser had received our medical reports and all was well. We've received the invitation to attend the panel and confirmed that we would be there. Less than a week to go now! We've managed to stay very calm so far, so let's hope we can keep it that way until Wednesday.

Sunday 7th March

On Friday we went to visit the fourth and last of the schools we shortlisted for H. It's quite similar in numbers and location to the one we visited on Thursday, but we were much more impressed with it. The children seemed to be happy there, and the person we spoke to asked all the right questions about H and took an interest in his educational and personal development so far. So we've narrowed down our list to the first school we saw, Mike's favourite, and the last one, my favourite, as it's local and the kids who attend it live in our street and surrounding area.

In the afternoon we drove to the town where H lives to visit his current school. The drive took a bit less time than we anticipated, and we ended up getting there just as the children were leaving to go home. We were supposed to arrive later to avoid meeting H. It was really weird seeing all these kids pouring out of the school in the uniform we've seen H wearing in the photos we've been given. I was desperately trying not to look, and not to be seen, but at the same time hoping to catch a glimpse! We did a quick u-turn and drove off to a nearby café.

At the right time we returned to the school and met with the Head, Annie and Sarah. We talked to them about the two schools we've shortlisted and they could see positive points about both. Sarah took notes and will get in touch with one of the LACESS (Looked After Children Education Support Service) people in our local authority to ask for their advice, but the final decision will be ours.

The head teacher was very friendly. She apologised on behalf of H's class teacher, who wanted to be present but couldn't be. We heard about H's behaviour when he first arrived and how it had improved thanks to all the work Annie and the school have put in. They told us about the strategies they used to deal with some of the more disruptive behaviours. He doesn't behave like that any more, but the possibility of regressing when (if) he joins us is very likely, so it would help us to use the same strategies they did. They gave us copies of his latest school and support reports and the foster carer gave us some more pictures, which are great.

We walked around the school and went into H's classroom. It was strange to be in a space where he is every week and to see his name on the wall and on his tray. They showed us his literacy and maths workbooks, so we got to see his handwriting. It was touching and special to see something so personal from the child we are hoping to adopt soon but have never met. We were there over two hours. We learnt so much about H and feel better prepared for when we eventually meet him – if everything goes OK at the matching panel on Wednesday.

To finish off a rather full day, we went to our friends Gavin and Sue's house. After a long wait, things are finally moving for them. They should be going to the panel and start introductions a couple of weeks after we do.

Tuesday 9th March

We spent the weekend putting together H's bedroom furniture so we could take pictures of his room and include them in the introductions book. We also put up a *Ben 10* poster. I sent Miranda a draft of the book and she liked it. We are hoping to record a DVD this weekend.

I think we're ready for the panel tomorrow. All the signs from the social workers are positive, and we've prepared the answers to the most obvious questions. We're still nervous but looking forward to it. Our lives will change tomorrow regardless of the outcome. The enormity of this is hard to describe. If it's a "no" we'll need to grieve for the loss of H and consider whether we can go through this again. If it's a "yes", then if all goes well with introductions and there's no further threat of impediment from the birth parents, we'll become dads to a six-year-old little boy. One thing we definitely have in common with him is that we've been waiting years to have a family. And tomorrow we find out if the wait is over.

This morning we received a "good luck" card from some friends and we are moved by how much support we have had; it's been amazing. Everyone is keeping their fingers crossed and waiting to hear from us tomorrow. I think this is partly because we've refused to give H's name to anyone, so our friends and family want the decision to be made so they can finally find out!

Wednesday 10th March

We surprised ourselves by sleeping well even though we were expecting to be up half the night with nerves. We set off for the town hall offices of the placing authority in plenty of time. Traffic was quite heavy and it took us half an hour longer than planned, so we made it literally just in time. Miranda was waiting for us with Sarah, H's social worker, his family finder and a trainee social worker, who we'd agreed could be present. The panel was running a few minutes late, so we had an opportunity to get ourselves together, as we'd got a bit stressed thinking we might be late and trying to find a parking space.

While we waited, we had an update about the birth family situation: they have written to the local authority to say that they think it's "not natural" for a boy to be brought up by two men and that it is in breach of the boy's human rights. This is coming from the people whose behaviour towards him led to his removal from their care! We're guessing his human rights weren't their priority at the time. The local authority didn't seem too concerned about it. They will write to them to explain what the situation is and what their options are: they can either go to court to challenge the placement order or accept the fact. We'll see.

The social workers were called into the panel meeting and five minutes later the panel adviser came to talk to us to make sure that we understood the process. She said that the social workers would be in for about thirty minutes and that the panel Chair would then come out, let us know what questions they wanted to ask us, and take us in to meet the panel members. Then she went in and we were left on our own. We went through the notes we had taken to prepare for any possible questions about Mike's family, gay adoption, attachment and bullying. After that, we just waited. Forty minutes after the social workers went in, the adviser came out again to let us know that the panel was being very thorough and it was taking a bit longer than expected, but they hoped to call us in soon. We didn't really know how to take the fact that it was taking longer than planned, but we tried to stay calm. Ten minutes later the panel Chair and the adviser came into the waiting room. They were very smiley, which was reassuring. They told us that everything was fine and that for the first time ever, the panel had no specific questions to ask other than why we thought this was a good match. They said that everything else had been addressed by our very thorough "adopters' views" report. Well worth the hours we put into writing it then!

We went into the panel room and were introduced to every member. There were twelve people around the table including the social workers, independent panel members, the medical adviser, an adopter, a foster carer (not H's), the legal adviser, a councillor, the note-taker, the panel adviser and the Chair. Like we'd been told, they asked us to comment on why we thought this was a good match and we told them what had attracted us to H when we saw his profile online, how every piece of information we'd read since had only made us more certain, and listed what we thought we can offer him: a stable relationship, one-to-one attention, a good support network, good training on attachment, and experience of children of a similar age though our volunteer work. Everyone nodded along and smiled – well, one of the members didn't smile at all but we tried to ignore her – and then we were given the opportunity to say anything else we thought we should say in support of the match. I started to say how much we wanted to offer H a good home but I got a bit emotional and couldn't finish, so Mike finished for me. After that we were asked to leave while they made their decision.

We were in the waiting room again and I felt so stupid for getting choked up! At this point Mike started crying. At least he had managed not to do it in front of the panel! A couple of minutes later the Chair, the adviser, and the social workers came to tell us that they were very happy to let us know that the panel was unanimously recommending approval for the match. I sort of went a bit numb after that. It was quite surreal to hear that something you've wanted so much is going to finally happen.

We were reminded that the panel's decision is only a recommendation and that the agency's "decision maker" would make the final decision within seven working days. They hastened to point out that the panel's recommendation is almost routinely accepted unless any new and relevant information comes to light.

We thanked everyone and agreed to deliver our introductions book and DVD to H's social worker by Monday. After everyone left, we grabbed a hot drink in the cafeteria with Miranda, who told us how the panel had taken longer than usual as H's permanence report was a bit out of date and they asked lots of questions about what had changed. Other than that there had been no major obstacles, just clarifications about Mike's family and the female role models in our network. We thanked her again for all her work and dedication and said goodbye.

We got in the car and I texted all our family members and friends while Mike drove. I then spent the whole journey back replying to congratulations. When we got home we rang our families and then went for a meal out to celebrate with some friends. We finally revealed H's name to everyone: Charlie.

We are incredibly happy. This is the moment we've been looking forward to for over two years. And it's coming true. We're going to be daddies!

Wednesday 17th March

I can't believe it's really been a week already since the panel. In some ways a lot has happened and in others not enough. After talking to parents with children in the two schools we liked best, we have chosen the first one we visited and applied for a place. We have also finished the introductions DVD and sent it together with the book and a puzzle we had made with our picture. This is because Charlie likes puzzles and it's meant to help him become familiar with our faces. The book has pictures of us and our families (grandparents, aunts and uncles, cousins), every room in our house (including several of what will be his room), the garden, our cars, the town where we live...and information about how long we've been together, our wedding day and favourite holidays. We've added little touches, like making sure that the pictures we've been given of Charlie can be seen in our living room. We're sending a copy of *And Tango Makes Three*, the book about the gay penguins who become parents, and we've also bought a penguin cuddly toy and placed it in several of the pictures. On the DVD we talk about ourselves, how much we're looking forward to meeting Charlie, and have filmed each other doing stuff we hope to do with him, like building Lego, doing puzzles, drawing, riding our bikes...We kept going into fits of laughter as we filmed it, so we've included an "out-take" section at the end (Miranda wasn't too sure about it, but we decided to go ahead with it).

I have been telling everyone at work and nobody suspected a thing, so there's been many a surprised face.

One of my colleagues "came out" as an adopter when I told her. She has mentioned her child before, but she's never told anyone at work that her child is adopted. It occurred to me that we can't really hide the fact that Charlie is adopted, unlike heterosexual couples. Well, people may wonder if he's the product of a previous relationship, but we're a lot more likely to be asked about it than a mum and dad out with their child.

I will be the one taking adoption leave. Mike's job can guarantee that he will have a job if he takes the leave, but not that he can come back to the same post. So that helped to make the decision. It's weird to think that I will be away from work for a few months. I'm actually looking forward to it! Charlie will be going to school shortly after he comes to live with us, so it was tempting to just be off work for three months – the time I'm on full pay – but because we don't know how well he will settle, I'll be requesting a whole year's leave with the option to go back early. At least we'll have that choice.

Thursday 18th March
As the date for introductions approaches – less than three weeks now – one big milestone is that Charlie has to be told he is moving on from his foster home to a new family. We talked to Annie, his foster carer, about this. Charlie has been in a home where he feels happy and safe. Why would he want to move? Annie assured us that Charlie has always known his current home is temporary, and as much as he likes it, he's really looking forward to moving on to his new family. He has been in that foster home for nearly three years, and he's seen other children move on to live with their new families. Apparently, when people visit the house, he tells them that he's hoping to be adopted soon.

In a recent conversation in the foster home, Annie explained to the children that a family could be a mum and a dad, or just one mum or one dad, two mums or two dads.

Annie told us that Charlie was intrigued by all these possibilities. A little girl who was in the same foster home went to a new family with two mums and apparently he liked the idea, so the foster carer has been doing some work about adoption by same-sex couples using some relevant pages from the book *Dad David, Baba Chris and Me*, which tells the story of a boy who is adopted by a male mixed-ethnicity couple. She also told us that the other day he said that he didn't think he liked the idea of having two dads, but when she told him that two dads meant two people to play football with, instead of one, he changed his mind! I guess this is something that she will work on more as she prepares to tell him about us and to show him our introductions book. That won't be until a few days before we meet him, so that his excitement and expectations can be managed.

Friday 19th March
It's St. Joseph's day, which in Spain is Father's Day, so it couldn't have been better timing when we got the call from Miranda this afternoon to tell us that the decision maker at the placing authority has confirmed the panel's recommendation for the match with Charlie. It's now official! Although we'd been told that it was almost certain that this would be the case, it was fantastic to have the confirmation. We should get a letter tomorrow or Monday, and shortly after we should get the official bit of paper that will allow us to apply for paternity and adoption leave from our employers. It's really happening!

Tuesday 23rd March
Mike took a call from Charlie's family finder. Charlie's birth mother has made a complaint to her MP, who has written to the local authority to enquire why Charlie is being placed with a gay couple. Last year another MP in the same local authority accused them of "kidnapping"

children to offer them for adoption. They will reply to the MP explaining their reasons for choosing us. This is really scary and I keep checking several national and local newspaper websites in case they go to the press...

Even though my last day at work is not until next week, today my co-workers arranged a surprise gathering. I received some gift vouchers and a lovely card, and many colleagues who couldn't make it sent emails with congratulatory messages and to wish us good luck. It was really sweet. It also meant a lot that I've been treated like any other member of staff who goes on maternity leave, even if it's adoption leave in my case.

Now that everyone at work knows, I've spent most of the day answering questions from colleagues about adoption. What most people found surprising is the fact that we've been matched with Charlie, yet we've never met him. I told them that you can't just parade potential parents in front of children, and the best way I found to explain the matching process is by comparing it to an arranged marriage. Parties from both sides (i.e. the social workers) decide that it's a good match, and once everything is set, that's when you meet. So you don't get together because you fall in love, instead you get together and then love grows as you get to know one another.

A friend of ours says that adoption is more like buying a house off a plan: you get to see the drawings, do all the paperwork, and only after you've bought it, you get to walk in and see it for real...

Monday 29th March

We're one week away from meeting our son! Today was my last day at work. It feels weird to think that I don't have a number of jobs waiting to be done, but it was great to write 'I won't be back until next year' on my out of office email auto-reply!

Today there was a bit of a panic as Charlie's social

worker is on holiday and nobody knew whether our introductions book and DVD had arrived. On Wednesday she will tell him that he's being placed with a family and then show him our book and DVD, so they need to be there. After a few hours of confusion, someone located them, so that was OK. We've also sent him a short story I wrote and illustrated about our road to adoption, and how we hope to make good dads for him; it also deals with the fact that he's going to have two dads and not a mum and dad. I wasn't really sure whether it was appropriate or not, but we showed it to Miranda last week and she liked it, so it went in the post this morning.

We've been in touch with the foster carer trying to sort out what to bring for introductions. She has suggested that as well as the cuddly penguin we've already agreed on, we should bring a Lego toy. That way, on the second or third day, we can sit down and build it together, which will give Charlie a chance to play with us but keep his distance if he needs to (as not a lot of eye contact is necessary). Apparently he's very good with Lego, so we'll be able to praise him on how well he does.

We've not heard any more about the enquiry from the MP so hopefully, with Easter around the corner, there won't be any delays to the introductions and placement plan.

We're off to Spain tomorrow for a few days. Since we probably won't be able to travel abroad until the adoption is completed and we can apply for a passport for Charlie, this may be our last visit this year. It will feel quite strange as I normally see my family every three months or so, but we hope they'll be able to visit us.

Friday 2nd April

Sarah, Charlie's social worker, went to visit him on Wednesday. She sent us an email to let us know how it went. We also spoke to Annie, his foster carer, who gave us her account. Sarah told Charlie she had news for him and could he guess what it might be. Charlie said 'No', but he clung to Annie and she could tell that he knew what was coming. Sarah told him they'd found new parents for him and he cried a little. Both Annie and Sarah think that this is a great sign as he's not bottling up his feelings, but it's still hard for us to hear. He was bound to feel a lot of mixed emotions about finally moving on to a new family and leaving Annie's home.

Sarah told him he would have two dads and showed him our book and puzzle. Apparently he was delighted with them. He liked the pictures of his room and the fact that Daddy Mike is a Beaver leader and he'll be able to join his group. He also liked the garden and he noticed all the pictures of him that we've placed all over the house. He was very impressed with that. He spotted Tango the penguin too. As soon as he'd seen the whole book he ran to Annie's husband to tell him all about it and share his news. He seemed really positive about having two dads, and that evening when he went to a school disco (I know, a school disco at six?) he told his best friend about it. They didn't show him the DVD at that point, but they did show him the story I wrote for him and apparently he loved it. In fact Annie told us she cried when she read it to him! When he went to bed he took his book with him. Both Sarah and Annie agree that it's gone as they hoped it would. He's nervous about meeting us next week, but Annie pointed out to him that we are nervous about meeting him too.

Annie also told us that the DVD we sent is among the best she's ever seen – although she probably says that to every adoptive parent – and she laughed at the collection of out-takes we included. Both Mike and I were welling up when we heard from Annie and Sarah. It's such a relief to know that Charlie's fine about having two dads and looking forward to meeting us. We may ring Annie again on Sunday to find out how he does once the news sinks in.

Saturday 3rd April

Still no news about the birth parents and their complaints. Today I wrote this letter, which I know I cannot send, to express what I'd like to say to them:

Dear birth parents,

We will meet Charlie very soon and if all goes well he will come to live with us and we will in time adopt him.

We know that you're angry about many of the things that have happened to Charlie in his short life. We know that you accept responsibility for some of those things, and that you blame other people for some of them. Now you've been told that he will be placed with a gay couple and you're angry. We're not sure if you're angry with us, social services, or yourselves. You feel that you need to do something and you've chosen to aim your anger at us.

We hope that we can address some of the concerns that we think you may have:

You're worried about Charlie, and we understand that. We wonder if you're worried that we will "teach" him to be gay. Both of us grew up with heterosexual parents and they didn't teach us to be gay, we just turned out that way. We don't believe that you can teach someone to be gay. Research on children brought up by gay or lesbian parents shows that Charlie is no more likely to grow up gay than any other child. He will be encouraged to develop friendships with boys and girls, and when it comes to relationships he will choose who he wants to be with. Like most boys, he will probably choose a girl. If that's the case, we will welcome it and hope he will be very happy with her.

Similarly, he will be encouraged to play with whatever he wants to play. We know he likes to play football and therefore we will support him and take him to football training and matches if that's what he wants to do. We will not make him play with dolls or dress him in pink outfits, if that's what you're worried about. He will play the same games as the other kids in his school and he will dress in the same clothes as the other kids.

We have lots of female friends and relatives and he will not be in a gay-only or male-only environment. We will make sure that he has plenty of positive female role models from among friends and family, neighbours and teachers. Some people say that a child needs a mother. He has a mother and a father. You two will always be that, even if he doesn't live with you. He will now have two more dads that he will live with.

During our adoption process we have been police-checked three times in the last two years. We have no convictions and we will never harm Charlie.

We wish we could meet you to explain this to you in person. And to ask you for maybe one of his baby photos, not for us but for him to keep. We also would like to know what he was like as a baby so that one day we can tell him. We would like to know if he's named after a relative or if there was a particular reason why you chose his name, which we won't change. We would like to see what you look like so that when he grows up we can tell him that he looks like you.

We will do our best for Charlie when he becomes our son. He will be looked after, supported, nurtured and loved. This we can promise you.

Monday 5th April

We're back from Spain now. We've received a letter from our local education authority confirming a place for Charlie in our chosen school, which is fantastic.

Miranda rang, even though it's a bank holiday! Charlie's family finder spoke to his birth parents. They had some questions and the family finder was able to answer them, so they feel reassured and even willing to meet us! Miranda thinks that part of the problem was that Sarah simply wrote them a letter to inform them that a gay couple was adopting Charlie instead of actually visiting them and explaining everything. We will meet them separately for thirty minutes each towards the end of introductions. We're not looking forward to it, as it won't be comfortable, but we really welcome the opportunity to ask them about Charlie, and to hear anything they can tell us about him.

Miranda also told us that our attachment-focused counselling will have to start after the placement now, as Charlie's local authority haven't arranged it yet. This is a pity, as we were meant to do a couple of sessions before meeting him.

In the evening we rang Annie to see how Charlie's been doing since he was told about us last Wednesday. A little boy picked up the phone and I was really thrown as I feared it might be Charlie. After a few seconds I managed to ask if Annie was in and she came to the phone laughing. She'd asked her grandson, who is staying with her, to answer the phone, and then remembered she'd asked us to ring, so she figured I must have thought it was Charlie. After that she told me that Charlie's last day at school on Thursday had been really emotional. He took the introductions book with him and showed it to his classmates at the end of the day. A lot of them cried and their mums and teacher cried too! He also had a long hug with his best mate and told him it was OK to be sad because it was a sad moment! Charlie cried quite a bit, but Annie was really pleased about this as only six months ago he'd have said he didn't care and he hated everyone anyway, so it showed how capable of attachment and expressing his feelings he's become.

One of his classmates asked him why he was moving to another family. Annie heard him reply that he couldn't live with his mummy and that's why he needed two daddies. Another boy apparently chipped in that having two dads was "gross". One can't help wondering if he heard that from his parents – clearly a six-year-old does not form such opinions, he repeats what he's heard at home. Charlie replied that it wasn't gross, and that he wanted two dads! On the one hand, I feel sad that he's had to experience such an encounter already, on the other, I'm incredibly proud of him for that response!

He's also been watching the DVD we made for him over and over and playing with the puzzle we sent him. When it's finished and our picture is complete he says to everyone 'these are my dads'. Annie told me he's now dropped our names and refers to us as Daddy and Dad. Apparently he's really at ease with the idea of two dads. He's been asking questions about his new school. She also mentioned that he's been tearful and clingy, because although he's excited about moving on to his new family, he's sad to go.

I told Annie how happy we were that they are Charlie's foster carers, since they've obviously done such a good job (they've actually won an award for their many years of outstanding foster care), and she said that she thought we were the best match for Charlie and she feels sure that Charlie will want to be with us. He has even said he wants to learn Spanish! He's learned to say "hola" and also, for some reason, how to say "lavadora" (washing machine). Does this mean he'll want to do the washing?

The updates from the foster carer have helped us to push aside the "what if he hates us?" anxiety we've been having as the date for introductions approaches. We're so excited. We're nervous about meeting him but really looking forward to it. Despite our nerves we will do our best to be ourselves. We know the first meeting is likely to be somewhat awkward and that's why we're "only" staying for two hours. Once we have got over the nerves and excitement of tomorrow we can start to get to know each other and do things together in a much more natural way. I don't know how much sleep we'll get tonight. Tomorrow we will meet our son for the first time and all our lives will definitely change forever. We just want everything to go well.

Tuesday 6th April

This morning we got up early and drove to the town where Charlie currently lives. We had a meeting with Sarah and she gave us a whole load of paperwork, including the care order, placement order, and a letter that allows us to authorise minor medical treatment for Charlie. Then we followed her to the foster carers' home. I was uncharacteristically calm and Mike was very nervous. As we pulled up we saw Charlie waving at us behind the glass front door, which took us by surprise. We waved back, parked the car, and went to the door with Sarah. He opened it for us and Sarah introduced us as Daddy Mike and Dad Pablo. We both said how nice it was to finally meet him and he was quite shy, almost hiding behind Annie's legs. He looked just like in the pictures, which I realise is a silly thing to say. We finally met Peter, Annie's husband. Both of them laugh all the time and their home is very welcoming. We went to the living room, where Charlie had started the puzzle with our picture. He finished it fairly quickly, which gave us an opportunity to praise him on how well and how quickly he'd done it. Then we played with a *Ben 10* 3D puzzle that was actually quite difficult. This allowed us to help him and genuinely work together to complete it. Annie mentioned that he's left-handed and I said I am left-handed too. It may seem silly but that really made me feel connected to him, something that we share, almost like it's something that I might have passed on to him if he were my birth son. Charlie seemed pleased to hear I was left-handed too, as if he was thinking the same thing.

Annie took a couple of pictures for his life story book, and with the excuse of posing for the pwictures asked him to give each of us a hug. It felt a bit forced, but it was our first hug! After that we helped him put together some paper planes. Annie praised him for his patience and not getting frustrated with the 3D puzzle and the planes, and mentioned how he used to get grumpy. He withdrew a little at that point, but I suggested that he show us his room and he quickly stood up and led us to it. He proudly showed us many of his toys, and Annie helped him to show us the chart Sarah's done for him with the introductions plan for the next two weeks. I asked him if he was ticklish and tickled his foot. His feet aren't ticklish at all! I said that I was and he felt comfortable enough to tickle my feet.

The two hours flew by and soon we were saying goodbye. We could tell he was getting a bit stressed by this time, so it was perfect timing. He gave us each a big hug and we left.

We are really pleased with how it went. We weren't sure how we would feel, and it was strange to meet him after everything we've read and heard. We didn't feel a "wave of love" come surging as soon as we saw him. And he didn't come rushing towards us when we first met. We think both these are good signs. We were nervous and so was he. And we simply do not know each other. We want to love him, and we will. It will come soon enough. We already feel like he's part of our lives. We can't wait to spend a lot more time with him and for our love for him, and his love for us, to grow.

Miranda rang us in the evening to ask how it went and to ask if we want to proceed. We said yes, of course, and she was very pleased. Tomorrow will be a much more "real" experience. We will have got over the nerves of the first meeting and it will feel more natural.

Post-script: April 2011

It's now a year since Charlie came to live with us. It's been interesting looking back as I re-read my diaries of our adoption and the first day we met him, as it seems like a lifetime ago. In my entry for that first day, I talked about not feeling an instant "wave of love" when we first met him. Within a few days we felt more and more connected and very soon he'd made a place for himself in our hearts. Two weeks after introductions started, Charlie moved in with us. The day we took him from his foster carers' home was very hard. We'd envisaged it as a happy day, the day we'd start our lives as a new family, but for Charlie it was the day he said goodbye to the happy home he'd lived in for the previous three years. We felt like we were snatching him away and we know it was really hard for Annie and Peter too.

We met both his birth parents. His birth father cross-examined us on how we were going to bring Charlie up. We put up with it to reassure him, but I just wanted to tell him that if he had such high expectations and ideas about how Charlie should be brought up maybe he should have done a better job himself! His birth mother was a lot more friendly and genuinely wanted to know that Charlie would be in a nice home. A few weeks after our meeting, Sarah brought us a letter from her. In the letter she said that she thought that we'd be good for Charlie, which was a very pleasant surprise. I wonder if she's more comfortable with us because Charlie has no "new" mum to compete with his memory of her. This may explain why his birth father is more against us. Charlie will never have another mum but he has two more dads to "replace" him.

Charlie adapted really quickly to his new school and hasn't had any problems there at all. He's doing well academically and hasn't needed any of the behavioural support he received at his previous school. Our first Christmas together was special, as was his "first" (actually seventh) birthday with us.

We've remained in touch with Annie and Peter, who in the first few months were an invaluable source of help and support. They've also been a great source of information about all the things we never thought to ask, and they have helped us to check out the truth about some of Charlie's "stories" about his past...

After three independent reviews, we applied for the adoption order in October. When he was informed of this, Charlie's birth father applied for leave of court to contest the placement order, which was worrying. However, at the hearing in December the judge dismissed his application, which Charlie's birth mother didn't support. In February we had our adoption day in court. This marked the end of the process and also the end of social worker visits! Losing Sarah was a welcome relief because her visits really upset Charlie, who was afraid she might take him away every time she came to see him, and he reacted with quite extreme behaviour. Miranda has actually stayed in touch even though we're no longer her responsibility. I have to say that even though we sometimes questioned some of her decisions and certainly wished she'd had more time for us, we're glad that she was our social worker. She did well for us at both the panels. Since Charlie was placed, she's been very supportive, and continues to be so although she could have washed her hands of us after the adoption was finalised.

I have to remind myself that Charlie's been with us for a relatively short time. It feels like he's lived with us forever, and sometimes it's hard to remember our lives without him. During the first few weeks Charlie tested a lot of boundaries as he learnt to trust us. He came from a very violent background, and as he regressed, as most adopted children do, there were a lot of behaviours to "un-learn". Some we've got over and some we're still working on. The attachment-focused counselling has been incredibly helpful to understand his feelings, to discuss and accept our own failings and learn to celebrate our successes as well. Some statistics say that a third of adoptions of children over five years of age disrupt, and it's true that at times it has been extremely hard going. But overall it's been everything we hoped for. As I look back, I see how far we've come. At the beginning we had a child whose behaviour was mostly motivated by his circumstances as an adopted child. Some of Charlie's behaviour will always be rooted in the traumatic events that led to his being removed from his birth family and being adopted, but I think most of his behaviour now is like that of any seven-year-old boy: testing and challenging authority as he develops his own personality. We are a family. It really doesn't matter to us that we missed out on the first six years of his life. In fact, most days we almost "forget" about it. It's not about the past, but about the present and the future. We need to be aware of his past to be able to accept and understand some of his behaviours, but on a day-to-day basis he is just Charlie, our son.

The adoption process is tough. But it is there for a reason. I think it takes a special kind of person to become an adopter. It takes a special kind of person to be a parent! Sometimes I think all parents-to-be, whether adoptive or birth parents, should go through an assessment of their competence to be parents and be made to read some of the books we've read. This thought crosses my mind every time I see a fifteen-year-old pushing a pram, or parents shouting at their children in the supermarket.

The fact that we were a gay couple trying to adopt had an impact on our decision-making, our assessment and approval, and – I think – mostly on the matching stage. I believe many family finders still want heterosexual adopters. I also believe our local authority "programmed" us to accept that as gay adopters we'd never be considered for a young child, and this was based on their own lack of experience of gay adopters. We were, after all, only the second gay couple they'd dealt with. Since our adoption, we've heard of lots of other gay couples being matched with much younger children. For us this is not a problem. We've got Charlie and he's our son. We wouldn't change a thing. But other prospective gay adopters who are faced with similar assumptions should challenge them.

One thing that sets us apart from heterosexual couples who adopt is the fact that, if the child they adopt matches their ethnicity, they have a choice about what they tell other people. We don't. People may wonder if Charlie's the product of a previous relationship, but in general most people assume he's adopted and ask about it. Charlie won't be able to hide his adoptive status and it's not his choice whom he tells.

As gay adopters we feel we need to go the extra mile. We're very aware that there are people out there who don't think gay people should be allowed to adopt; people who want us to fail. There aren't any statistics available on the successful adoption rate among gay and lesbian adopters, and we want to make sure we're not the ones who provide ammunition for the haters. I think this makes us more determined to succeed, but it also puts extra pressure on us to be "perfect dads".

With regards to being gay parents, there are two more issues I want to address: how Charlie feels about having two dads and our experience of how others feel about Charlie having two dads.

I'll start with the latter. We've not experienced any hostility from school, neighbours or passers-by. When Charlie started at his new school we worried about how other kids and their parents might react. We made a point of making sure both of us dropped him off or picked him up, sometimes on our own and sometimes together. We spotted a couple of looks as parents saw us together and it dawned on them that both of us are Charlie's dads. No nasty looks, though, more the look of a light bulb switching on as they put two and two together. The other children just accepted that Charlie has two dads. Some of the parents later told us that their children had asked why that was, and had been satisfied with the answer that some people have a mum and a dad, others have one parent and a few have two mums or two dads. In fact a single mum told me that she and her children had a negative image of dads, so it was wonderful to see Charlie have not one, but two involved dads who look after him!

Some day we will have to sit down and explain to Charlie what "gay" means and that some people have prejudices against two men or two women being a couple, just like some people have prejudices based on race, religion, or where you were born. We will also have to explain that some people think that gay people shouldn't bring up children. And we will have to arm him with really good responses and strategies to deal with any name-calling, rejection or awkward conversations.

We often go to the local park after school. One day, two of the dads were teaching a few of the boys how to head a football and they were having a great time – both the dads and the kids. I couldn't help wondering if Charlie feels let down by Mike and me when it comes to football. When they told him he was going to have two dads he probably thought he'd get two men who'd teach him football tricks and love to kick a ball around. Instead he's got us. Mike can't kick a ball for toffee and I do my best but Charlie knows I'm not very good at it. Still, we can't be perfect and, as he will no doubt tell us in his teens, all fathers are a disappointment at some point or other.

With regards to how Charlie feels about having two dads, he has on a couple of occasions (especially around Mothers' Day) said that he wanted a mum and dad. When we asked him why, he replied that 'everyone else has a mum and dad'. We went through the people he knows who have two dads, two mums, or single parents. I reminded him that just because he doesn't live with her doesn't mean that he doesn't have a mother any more. I then pointed out to him that, when you think about it, he actually has one mum and three dads. 'And I don't think anyone at school can beat that!' I added. He seemed quite pleased about that. We also asked him if he thought there was anything that a mum and dad could give him that we can't. He said that there's nothing wrong with having two dads, but it's just not what he wanted. Unable to come up with anything else, we told him that he'll understand one day.

I don't think what Charlie said is an argument against gay adoption, but an argument for more clarity when explaining adoption to children in care. There is an inconsistency in the system. Adopters can be couples or single, regardless of their sexual orientation, but children in care are not made aware that single or gay adopters could become their family. This means that they build up a picture in their heads of a new family with a mum and a dad. It then becomes a question of unmet expectations for children, who are disappointed, not because their new family isn't good enough, but because it's not what they imagined. There is also an element of wanting to be like everyone else. Children of Charlie's age don't want to stand out. Unfortunately, from the moment he went into care, he stopped being like everyone else.

We have had to explain to Charlie that two men can be in a loving relationship. We had to tell him that, even though in most cases a man and a woman are in love, sometimes it's two men or two women. When the issue came up, it was surprising because we always assumed that he understood our relationship. He'd seen our wedding pictures, Mike and I give each other a kiss when we leave the house or come home, and we sleep in the same bed, which he sees when he comes to wake us up. Looking back, his foster carer and social worker talked to him about having two dads, but not about the fact that those two dads were a couple!

I have to acknowledge the amazing support that New Family Social, the gay and lesbian adopters' charity, has been. Not only in providing an online forum for discussion, but with their get-togethers and their annual camping trip. We socialise with a whole variety of people and the vast majority of our friends are heterosexual couples and their children, but at the New Family Social events Charlie can meet other children who have gay and lesbian adoptive parents. This is fantastic for him as he can see that not only are many other kids adopted, but they also have two dads or two mums, so he's not so different after all.

That, I guess, is my ending: none of our worries and fears about bringing up a child as a gay couple (will he resent it? Will other people reject us or him? Can we do it?) have materialised. I feel like writing to everyone who opposes gay adoption, including some family finders, and saying 'See? We adopted a boy and he's happy. We're happy. There's one less child in the care system. A family has come together and civilisation hasn't collapsed. The world hasn't ended.'

join the adoption revolution